How to Write Great Business Cases

*To our respective parents who nourished our love of learning
and storytelling.*

How to Write Great Business Cases

Karin Schnarr

Associate Professor, Strategic Management, Lazaridis School of Business & Economics, Wilfrid Laurier University, Canada

Meredith J. Woodwark

Associate Professor, Organizational Behaviour and Human Resource Management, Lazaridis School of Business & Economics, Wilfrid Laurier University, Canada

Cheltenham, UK • Northampton, MA, USA

Published by
Edward Elgar Publishing Limited
The Lypiatts
15 Lansdown Road
Cheltenham
Glos GL50 2JA
UK

Edward Elgar Publishing, Inc.
William Pratt House
9 Dewey Court
Northampton
Massachusetts 01060
USA

Paperback edition 2024

A catalogue record for this book
is available from the British Library

Library of Congress Control Number: 2023937055

This book is available electronically in the **Elgar**online
Business subject collection
http://dx.doi.org/10.4337/9781803920658

ISBN 978 1 80392 064 1 (cased)
ISBN 978 1 80392 065 8 (eBook)
ISBN 978 1 0353 4450 5 (paperback)

Printed and bound by CPI Group (UK) Ltd, Croydon, CR0 4YY

Contents

Figures

Tables

About the authors

Karin Schnarr is an Associate Professor of Strategic Management at the Lazaridis School of Business & Economics, Wilfrid Laurier University, in Waterloo, Canada. Dr Karin Schnarr received her PhD in Strategic Management from the Richard Ivey School of Business at the University of Western Ontario in 2015. Dr Schnarr has written and published award-winning cases through a number of academic journals, case publishing outlets, and textbooks. She is a regular contributor to Harvard Business Publishing: Education on case-based learning and has presented on case writing, case innovation, and case-based research at numerous peer-reviewed international academic business conferences. Dr Schnarr leads the Strategy and Policy Track at the North American Case Research Association, the pre-eminent global organization for academic case writing, and is on the Editorial Advisory Board for The CASE Journal. She lives in Kitchener with her husband, Josif, and their incredible daughters, Alexis and Morgan.

Meredith J. Woodwark is an Associate Professor of Organizational Behaviour and Human Resource Management at the Lazaridis School of Business & Economics, Wilfrid Laurier University, in Waterloo, Canada. Dr Meredith Woodwark received her PhD in Organizational Behaviour from the Richard Ivey School of Business at the University of Western Ontario in 2015. Dr Woodwark has written and published numerous popular and award-winning cases in the organizational behaviour and leadership area in leading academic journals and case publishing houses. She is on the Editorial Board of the *Case Research Journal*, the premier academic case journal, and is on the Board of the North American Case Research Association. For the past eight years, Dr Woodwark has been a regular panelist on case-based learning and case innovation at peer-reviewed international academic business conferences. She lives in Stratford with her husband, Tristan, and their intrepid dog, Midnight.

Preface

The first purpose of this book is to help fellow academics develop their case research and writing skills to the point where they can complete great cases that meet their personal goals. For many, that will mean that their cases can be published in their chosen outlets. For others, that will mean that they can write cases that fill gaps in their course syllabus or that they can use as a final exam. There are plenty of valid reasons for wanting to know how to write a great case. For those of you who wish to publish your cases, getting your case published is great, but publishing cases that are used by instructors and students around the world is even better. Hence, our second purpose is to help readers seeking to publish their cases also develop the necessary skills to identify what makes a case attractive and valuable to users.

Whether you are a graduate student, professor or academic practitioner just starting to write cases or someone who has already written several, we are confident that the techniques we share in this book will help you take your case research to the next level. We are delighted to share everything we know about case research and writing, a discipline that has both challenged us and been a lot of fun for the past decade. We believe case research is a field of enormous growth potential, so we plan to enjoy the challenge and fun for as long as we can. Along the way, we hope to convince colleagues and students to join the case research club. The more people who participate in case research, the more its unique and critical contributions to management education will be recognized. Our personal goal in writing this book is to convince our readers to become active case researchers too. Herein we have given you all the tools to get started. Happy case writing!

Karin Schnarr and
Meredith J. Woodwark
November 2022

Acknowledgements

Looking back at how this book came to be, we could sum it up as a story of two like-minded people doing the right thing, at the right place, and at the right time. After the Academy of Management (AOM) conference in 2021, Edward Elgar editor Ellen Pearce was looking for an author to write the next volume in the academic 'How To Guides' series to be focused on case writing. We had been at AOM talking about case writing for the better part of a decade by that point, so she approached us to write the book, the timing was right, and the result is this volume. Although Francine O'Sullivan from Elgar later took over publishing this project assisted by Beatrice McCartney, we are grateful to them all for trusting this volume to us, and for the opportunity to codify all of our case writing knowledge into this guide so we can share what we have learned with current and aspiring case writers.

We were fortunate enough to meet and complete our doctoral degrees at the Ivey Business School at Western University in London, Ontario. We both arrived at Ivey with a love of stories and degrees in English Literature as well as in Management. Lucky for us, Ivey was and continues to be a major proponent of and contributor to the case method in management education. There we had the unique opportunity to learn about case writing as part of our formal programme in management pedagogy from Dr Debbie Compeau. We each had prolific case writers as dissertation supervisors who both encouraged our interest in case writing, Dr Glenn Rowe and Dr Gerard Seijts respectively. Many staff members at Ivey Publishing helped us to publish our first few cases and encouraged us to keep at it since the process was a positive experience for newbie case writers.

After becoming hooked on case writing at Ivey, we then explored case conferences where we found developmental reviewers and helpful colleagues who pushed us to improve our work. Initially, we learned a lot at the case track of the Administrative Sciences Association of Canada (ASAC), and later we broadened our horizons by joining the North American Case Research Association (NACRA). At NACRA we were fortunate enough to meet and be trained by Dr Anne Lawrence of the Case Research Foundation from whose generous fellowships we each benefited. At NACRA we were also introduced to the *Case Research Journal* (CRJ) and the tremendous expertise of the former editor, Dr Gina Grandy, and the current editor (and fellow Ivey grad), Eric Dolansky. We are very appreciative of the guidance, feedback, and encouragement we have received from the NACRA and CRJ community about all our case writing efforts. While there are too many people to list, we would like to call out Dr Anne Lawrence, Dr Eric Dolansky, Dr Michael Goodman, Dr Maria A. Ballesteros-Sola, and Dr John D. Varlaro for their early endorsements of this book.

In another stroke of luck, we landed at the same business school, the Lazaridis School of Business & Economics at Wilfrid Laurier University, where we have also found substantial support for our case writing contributions as well as many faculty colleagues who share our love for cases. At Lazaridis we had fantastic opportunities to grow as case writers, including the opportunity to work on live cases, to teach graduate students and our colleagues how to write cases, to publish many cases, to be responsible for case tracks at ASAC and NACRA, to try our hand at special editing an issue of CRJ, and of course to write this book.

We have also had the opportunity to work with colleagues both from the Lazaridis School and Ivey as well as other international academic institutions on numerous presentations on case writing and research at the Teaching and Learning Conference which is held every year as part of the Academy of Management. We have been so fortunate to have wonderful presentation colleagues, Dr Karen McMillan and Dr Brent Beal, who have been our partners in helping to spread the word about great case writing, live cases, and working with students in co-creating cases. And a thank you to the leadership of the Teaching and Learning stream at AOM for being so supportive of case learning, writing, and research. These collaborations with Karen and Brent also led a number of years ago to the development and publishing of a book on student-written, instructor-facilitated cases which is a great guide for instructors who would like to bring case writing into their classrooms at any level!

Lastly, but most importantly, we thank our families, Joe, Alexis, and Morgan, and Tristan and Midnight, for keeping us entertained, fed, loved, and walked throughout the book writing process.

Abbreviations

AAA	American Accounting Association
AABRI	Academic and Business Research Institute
AABS	Association of African Business Schools
ABA	Allied Business Academies
AEMBA	Association des Étudiants MBA
AIMA	All India Management Association
AOM	Academy of Management
ASAC	Administrative Sciences Association of Canada
AUC	American University Cairo
BALAS	Business Association of Latin American Studies
CCMP	Centrale de Case et de Médias Pédagogiques
CEEMAN	The International Association for Management Development in Dynamic Societies
CEIBS	China Europe International Business School
CLADEA	Latin American Council of Management Schools
CRF	Case Research Foundation
CRJ	Case Research Journal
EFMD	European Foundation for Management Development
HBP	Harvard Business Publishing
HEC	Hautes études commerciales
IBIMA	International Business Information Management Association
ICI	Index Copernicus International
ICIS	International Conference on Information Systems
ICRC	Indian Case Research Centre
IFCR	Institute of Finance Case Research
IM	Instructor's Manual
IM/TN	Instructor's Manual or Teaching Note

IMD	International Institute for Management Development
IP	Ivey Publishing
IRB	Institutional Review Board
ISCAP	Information Systems and Computing Academic Professionals
MBAA	Midwest Business Administration Association
MENA	Middle East and North Africa
MIT	Massachusetts Institute of Technology
NACRA	North American Case Research Association
NJP	Neilson Journals Publishing
PARCC	Program for the Advancement of Research on Conflict & Collaboration
RSM	Rotterdam School of Management
SCR	Society for Case Research
SHRM	Society for Human Resource Management
SWIF	Student-written, instructor-facilitated
TCJ	The CASE Journal
TLC	Teaching and Learning Conference, Academy of Management
TN	Teaching Note
WCA	Western Casewriters Association

1. Why write a business case?

We have each been writing and publishing business cases for over a decade. Together, we conservatively estimate that we have written, published, supervised, or presented approximately four dozen cases. If we include completed case reviews, that number easily doubles. In addition, we present to various conference audiences several times per year about how to write cases, how to supervise others writing cases, and how to use cases in novel ways such as live cases. As scholars, we devote an inordinate amount of time and energy to a practice that most would label *writing business cases*. While it is true that our practice produces written cases, we prefer the term *case research* for many reasons which will become apparent throughout the book – not the least of which is that when we have finished writing the case document itself, we are necessarily less than halfway through the full scope of work involved in completing a business case.

In our experience, it is common for scholars who have not published cases to underestimate the amount of work and the skill sets involved in producing superior cases. While non-case writing academics correctly expect that case writers must be excellent writers, they often fail to understand that they must also be strong scholars in their fields as well as talented instructors. Case research is a unique set of scholarly skills that combines organizational research and storytelling into case writing, together with mastery of the applicable disciplinary theory and literature along with a pedagogically sound presentation in the instructor's manual (IM) or teaching note (TN).[1] Moreover, both the case and the IM/TN documents must be internally consistent to facilitate instructor effectiveness and maximize student learning. It is worth underscoring from the start that – unless you do not want to publish – when you undertake to write a business case you are almost always committing to writing two separate but complementary documents that together constitute one publication: a case document for use by students and instructors; and an IM/TN for instructor use only. The terminology gets confusing because the term *case* from the student's perspective is the only document that they are supposed to see, whereas from the author's perspective publishing a *case* means having both documents accepted by the publisher, the second of which is only accessible by instructors.

At this point, you may be getting the correct impression that writing cases – or case research as we prefer to call it – is not as straightforward as you may have initially thought. In fact, you may be wondering why any academic would complete two full documents only to be credited with one publication! You would be right to observe that for that reason alone, case research is undervalued in academia relative to other forms of scholarly publishing. In a competitive field like academia where the number and quality of publications count for so much of a scholar's career success, plenty of academics will question why we choose to devote a substantial portion of our scholarly careers to case research.

We will outline our arguments for the importance of case research in detail, but the short answer for now is that writing business cases is an incredibly impactful scholarly activity. When you publish a case that becomes a best-seller, it means that tens of thousands of business students and instructors in dozens of countries around the world are learning from your work each year. Even cases that are not top sellers can have thousands of readers around the world every year. Other than best-selling textbooks or popular business books, it is difficult to exceed the scale of impact that case research affords scholars. Only the very most well-read journal articles, books, or book chapters attain anywhere close to the scale of impact of cases. If it is motivating to you to know that a large number of business instructors and students are using your work on a regular basis, incorporating a case research practice into your academic career may be as professionally gratifying for you as it has been for us.

Whether you are new to case research or whether you are looking to learn more, our goal with this book is not only to get you started – or further along – writing business cases, but also to help you develop or deepen a practice of case research that will give you the best chance of a series of successful case publications in a range of outlets. We will share why we do case research, how we do it, outline all the interesting choices and decisions to be made throughout the process, and be honest about all the practical lessons we have learned along the way. We want you to get your work published so you can get academic recognition for all your work, and so that students and instructors around the world are able to learn from your efforts and expertise. In short, we want to show you how you too can have global impact in business and management education through case research. We note that while we focus on business cases for management education, much of what we discuss in this volume about case research is also applicable to writing cases for related fields (e.g., healthcare management).

WHAT IS A BUSINESS CASE?

Fundamentally, a case – sometimes called a teaching case – is a pedagogical tool or resource typically used for a brief period such as a single class session. The case document serves as the basis for a discussion-based analysis of the case data by the class instructor and students, the purpose of which is to achieve the learning objectives for the session as laid out in the IM/TN. Some instructors or institutions rely exclusively on the case method. In that instance, each course only has a set of cases, also called a case package, instead of a text-book so that the course learning objectives are met entirely via cases. Others combine the use of textbooks and readings with cases, so the course learning objectives are achieved using multiple resources. It is important to note that the recent move towards online education due to the COVID-19 pandemic has shown that the case method can be conducted entirely virtually, although traditionally it has been done primarily in person.

For several reasons, the meaning of the term *case* can be confusing because it has different meanings depending on the usage. Coming from a student's perspective, a case means only the document used to guide class discussion without any of the analysis or solutions. When an author publishes a case, the case document itself is openly published, while the IM/TN is made available only to qualified instructors interested in the case. This ensures students do not have the suggested answers to the case prior to the case discussion in class. Both components are required to publish your case, but the IM/TN is effectively published and provided only for those with restricted access. A published case typically refers to the combined set of two documents: the case, and the accompanying IM/TN.

Lastly, we note that the term *case study* is sometimes used interchangeably with the term *case*. For instance, in some parts of Europe what we call a case is referred to as a case study by regional convention. In our opinion, this usage of the term *case study* causes confusion between the case method as a pedagogi-cal method and the case study method as a qualitative research method, which clearly has a quite different purpose from what we mean by a business case. Therefore, we reserve the term *case study* to denote the qualitative research method and use exclusively *case* or *business case* for the pedagogical business cases we are discussing in this book.

The rest of the definition of a case depends on what type of case is being considered. But before we outline the diverse types of cases, we first need to understand why the case method is so prevalent in management education.

WHY CASES ARE USED IN MANAGEMENT EDUCATION

Essentially, the case method is vicarious learning through storytelling. The case method has been used in business schools for approximately a century now since their early adoption at Harvard University. The underlying assump-tion behind the case method is that students learn more and better using an active, participatory, and reflective approach to learning rather than a passive one. While there are plenty of variations, the typical way cases are used is to assign the case document to the class along with case analysis questions to be prepared in advance for a particular class session. All students are expected to read and analyse the case, prepare their answers to the assigned questions, and come to class ready to explain their analysis, recommended decision, and associated rationale. For a comprehensive review of the case method from a student perspective, see Wood et al. (2018).

The case instructor guides the class through the case facts and questions by eliciting contributions from prepared students. The instructor may also include explanations about important concepts or theories that apply to the case and may introduce challenges to the students' way of thinking about the focal issue. Ideally, a good case prompts a lively debate about the best course of action for the protagonist. Often, a case class ends with the instructor revealing the actual decision the protagonist made along with the resulting outcome. The case method process challenges students' critical thinking and problem-solving skills as they must analyse the case data and develop effective solutions (Herreid, 2004). Students learn to make decisions by practising the decision-making process from the protagonists' point of view in a safe class-room environment. Students also develop communication skills in explaining their ideas and reasoning to the class, and by listening to others' arguments. The participatory nature of the case method helps students be more engaged and self-directed in their learning and studies. All these skills are helpful once students graduate into their management careers. Cases are one of the primary tools for closing the familiar research–practice gap where there is little communication between academic researchers and business practitioners; cases can both bring new business practices into the research realm and introduce new applications for research.

However, the case method is not without its criticisms. Cases can become dated quite quickly so that the focal question, product, or business model no longer seems relevant to students. For example, current undergraduate business students do not remember when Netflix delivered movies through mailed DVDs as opposed to home streaming, making it difficult for them to relate to cases from that period. Cases are also difficult to use effectively when the focal decision is already known to the class, which can easily happen in our era of 'googling'. Some instructors argue that cases are unrealistic and over-simplified compared to real-life organizational decision-making. Others believe that the lessons from a specific case are not generalizable, so the value of studying a particular case does not enhance future knowledge or skills. Finally, some critics believe that students do not learn much from case analyses and often find them unengaging because they know that the work they put into the case will have no impact on the focal organization; hence, cases can become unmotivating when they are only for their own sake. Many of the new alternative case formats including short cases, multi-media or graphic cases, and live cases aim to address these criticisms while maintaining the key benefits of the case method.

DECISION-BASED CASES

There is no definitive typology of case types or list of accepted definitions. In our research, we have found that there are distinct kinds of cases based on the case purpose, the source type, as well as the case format. Below we will outline the different case types beginning with the most common case type and the main focus of this book: the decision-based narrative case.

The vast majority of business cases used in management education are decision-based or decision-focused cases; hence, this type of case is the primary focus of this book. When we are talking about cases or business cases, we are referring to decision cases unless otherwise specified. A decision case is a type of case that outlines the context and supporting data about a key managerial decision to be made by the case protagonist who must make and justify the decision. Note that in reality, the actual decision has already been made, since a case describes a past decision point in a real organization that has since moved on. The decision to be made in the case is often called the focal case question or issue. In traditional case analysis, students and instructors are limited to using only the data provided in the case to decide which course of action is the best; no outside sources are used. The focal case question in a decision case is based on actual, factual events and all the supporting data consists of verified facts. The idea is to place students in the role of the protagonist with the same information available at the time and simulate the process of deciding between mutually exclusive options. By way of examples, we have written a case about a convenience store chain manager who must decide how to revamp the business to compete as the industry shifts (see Woodwark et al., 2020b), a case about a manager who hired a friend and must decide whether or not to let him go (see Risavy and Woodwark, 2020), a case about an artificial intelligence marketing firm deciding whether to pursue a diverse hiring strategy (see Woodwark and Risavy, 2020), and a case about an international fast food company deciding how to pivot to stay successful (see Schnarr and Rowe, 2014). Decision cases focus in on a specific decision point that an individual, a group, an organization or firm, or even a group of organizations actually faced at a particular point in time. The outcome from using a decision-based case is that students thoroughly understand the pros and cons of each option and can provide a clear rationale for their recommended course of action.

We note that some authors distinguish between decision cases and problem cases (Ellet, 2007; 2018), the latter being cases where students must first determine the underlying root issue(s) because the case facts do not state it outright. While we recognize that the problem diagnosis step is important for case analysis and increases the difficulty level of the case, in our view such cases are nevertheless decision cases because once the diagnosis is complete, students must still decide on the best course of action to resolve the problem. Hence, we consider problem cases that do not define the key issue for students to be a more challenging form of decision case appropriate for more advanced students.

The goal in writing a good case is to prompt student debate about the best course of action. Learners must justify their choice using case data and consider the arguments of those in the class who have made an alternative choice. Therefore, the decision options given in the case cannot be too obvious and must all have sufficient benefit to be seriously considered. If the optimal decision is too evident or the merits of certain options too biased, the quality of the class discussion will suffer and stunt student learning.

One key point to understand about decision cases is that the same focal decision can be used to pursue different learning objectives depending upon on the perspective selected by the author in the IM/TN. Many focal decisions in organizations have a broad range of business implications; well-developed cases and IM/TNs have carefully selected topics for the case analysis linked to learning objectives and business theory. A case about the same focal decision in an organization written by a marketing professor may have similar case data as a case written by an organizational behaviour professor, but the core issues, learning objectives, and analysis outlined in the IM/TN will be quite divergent. Therefore, in order to truly understand what a decision case is intended to be about, instructors need to review the accompanying IM/TN to understand the specific learning objectives the case was designed to achieve.

Each business case has at least one level of analysis which is the perspective from which the focal case issue is analysed. This can include the industry, organization, team or group, and individual levels. Various business disciplines typically focus on certain levels of analysis for the case questions. For instance, strategic management scholars typically write cases asking students to decide what the firm or organization – or a subsection thereof – should do, whereas organizational behaviour scholars typically write cases about the decisions individual managers, groups, or organizations should make. The choice of level of analysis of the focal case question relates to the learning objectives the case is designed to achieve. For example, a case about how to respond to major changes within an industry could examine the question from an individual career planning perspective (individual level), or from a firm strategic perspective (organizational level). Both versions would include common data about the current and future state of the industry, but the former would include data about the protagonist's career to date and future goals, whereas the latter would include data about the firm's past performance within the industry and its future aspirations.

There are two main kinds of decision cases based on the nature of the empirical data used: primary source cases and secondary source cases. In both types of cases, some of the data can be disguised to protect confidential information provided by the focal organization. Although much less common, decision-based cases can also be hypothetical cases which are based on fictional rather than real data (see below).

Primary Source Cases

Primary source cases are based on direct research from people who participated in the focal case decision at the firm and who contribute original data to the case itself. For case research, most primary data are in the form of interviews, but other forms could include surveys or questionnaires, internal documents and communications such as reports or emails, and financial records that are not public. Some case journals will also accept sworn court documents or congressional hearings as primary sources. In a primary source case, much of the data will come from your case protagonist, although it is always wise to supplement and verify the data through other sources as well. Authors of primary source cases can also enhance the case data by using secondary sources as well (see Woodwark et al., 2020a). The various case journals and publishing outlets have different definitions about what data sources are considered primary vs. secondary data so it is always wise to check with your target outlet to be sure.

Each institution has its own rules about whether primary case research requires ethics or Institutional Review Board (IRB) ethics review prior to beginning to conduct external outreach to obtain primary data. Be sure to know the ethics approval expectations at your institution before you start collecting primary data.

Some case outlets publish only primary source, decision-based cases, so be sure to check the requirements of your target outlet before submitting. Finally, all reputable case outlets will require a representative from the subject organization to sign off on your case document prior to publication; the IM/TN does not require sign-off from the company. This is a crucial step because it also protects the case author once the case is published, especially if the leadership at the focal organization changes.

Primary source cases provide a richness of data because case authors can get details which are often not available through secondary source research (see Woodwark et al., 2020b, and Snowdon et al., 2014). They provide the opportunity to insert quotations from case protagonists which make the case format and flow more dynamic. There can also be an opportunity to include multiple voices in the case which provide alternative perspectives, more accurately mirroring what occurs during organizational decision-making (see Schnarr et al., 2021). Finally, primary source cases are often more engaging than those relying solely on secondary sources as students are more easily able to insert themselves into the action of the case.

The challenge with primary source cases is to make sure that the case does not read like a commercial for the organization or situation. This can sometimes be tricky to manage, given the need for the organization to sign off on the case prior to publication. If the case topic is more controversial, the organization may decide, once the case is completed, that they no longer wish to have the case published, or ask for the case narrative to be made more neutral. Those can be tricky situations for a case writer and one of the most challenging elements of writing a primary source case. It is always a good idea to be open and transparent with your company contact so that everyone is clear about the focus of the case. Sadly, many authors learn the hard way that obtaining sign-off on a case requires actively managing their relationship with the case contact through continual communication with the organization. An effective way to minimize surprises is to keep sharing case outlines and drafts through the writing process to try to reduce the risk that the organization might not give permission to publish.

Secondary Source Cases

Secondary source cases are those that are based only on available publicly published sources about the case focal issue, the protagonist and organization, and the industry. Sources should be reputable and include company websites and other publications, journalism such as newspapers, magazines and published interviews (e.g., television, radio, podcasts), industry reports and market research, social media, and court or legal records. The key challenge with secondary source cases is to find sufficient available data to build a workable case and to keep meticulous records about all your source materials.

Secondary source cases do not require approval from the protagonist or organization to be published; hence, they play a vital role in ensuring that potentially negative topics (which might not otherwise get approved) can be made into published cases (see MacMillan and Woodwark, 2016). Focal case questions involving corporate scandals or organizational failures typically must be developed as secondary source cases. Cases involving current issues covered in the news can often make for interesting secondary source cases that can be completed promptly while the issue is still on the minds of students and instructors provided sufficient information is available. However, sometimes you cannot find sufficient sources for the case you want to write and so authors may need to pivot to a different focal case question based on data availability. This is particularly true if cases are on small or medium-sized businesses or not-for-profit organizations where there is less availability of public data compared to publicly traded companies.

Students love to read and analyse cases on organizations they know and whose products they use (e.g., Apple, Starbucks, Tesla, and McDonald's). Secondary source cases work very well when cases are focused on large, multinational, well-known companies where it could be difficult to gain the official approval of the legal or communications department for publication (see Schnarr and Rowe, 2014).

Disguised Cases

Both primary and secondary source cases are sometimes disguised, meaning that the actual names of the person, firm, or even industry outlined in the case are not revealed to readers upfront; rather, the disguised elements are assigned fake information instead. Although disguised cases are based on real data, the fake information enables a class discussion that would not otherwise be possible to have since students are too familiar with the outcome or the people involved. Using the fake information, the case is still written so that the case data parallels the actual events without giving the specific context away (see MacMillan and Woodwark, 2012). A famous example of a case disguise is *Carter Racing* (Brittain and Sitkin, 2008), which secretly parallels the issues the National Aeronautics and Space Administration (NASA) faced in the 1986 *Challenger* disaster. The true source of the case data is only revealed to students after the analysis has been completed so students can assess whether they make the same decision-making errors as NASA. The case disguise technique can also be used when the subject company is willing to tell their story but is hesitant to divulge their name publicly. It is also important to recognize that the whole case does not need to be disguised. For example, when companies are not comfortable disclosing their current financial position, multipliers are often used so that the financial data maintains the same ratio proportions while protecting the confidentiality of the actual organizational performance. Using a disguise can sometimes enable authors to publish a case despite the company getting cold feet prior to sign-off.

Hypothetical Cases

The defining characteristic of a hypothetical case is that it is not based on real events but rather is a fictitious story to illustrate a particular issue. While they may appear disguised because the names can seem fictionalized, in a hypothetical case the entire story is fictional too. Hypothetical cases are not as prevalent as primary or secondary source cases as many case journals and publishing outlets will not accept them. Often, a hypothetical case is used because the issue being explored is not one that has been documented or one where it would be difficult to obtain primary or secondary data. For instance, cases about common ethical decisions are often hypothetical with invented protagonists, actions, and organizations, but they are recognizable as scenarios that do occur and are worthy of class discussion because the issues are generalizable.

Hypothetical cases are also often used for student assignments or exams, or for use by individual instructors in their own classrooms. With few exceptions, hypothetical cases are not typically publishable unless the outlet is in a specific domain such as accounting, ethics, or human resources, or the case is being written for a textbook.

NON-DECISION-BASED CASES

In our experience, the majority of cases used in business schools are decision cases where the outcome is a recommended decision and rationale; however, there are other purposes for using cases besides decisions. We will outline the following variations so you are familiar with these different uses should you ever encounter them. Depending on the topic, these variations can also be written using primary and/or secondary data or can be hypothetical cases.

Descriptive Cases

The purpose of a descriptive case is different from a decision case. A descriptive case is meant only to illustrate or show students how the concepts they have learned can be applied in a real-world example (Naumes and Naumes, 2015). For instance, textbooks often use descriptive cases at the start or end of text chapters to illustrate how a particular firm has applied the concepts or dealt with the issues in the chapter. Descriptive cases help students to see how what they are learning in the text chapter can be used by people in the workplace. This type of case is helpful for students who are in the preliminary stages of learning how to translate theories and concepts into application, and so the scope and complexity of a descriptive case tends to be limited to the key concepts in a specific chapter. Descriptive cases are meant to enhance understanding of the concepts to be learned so students understand how they relate to the illustrative example. These cases do not ask students to make evaluations or decisions about the information, nor to apply the concepts to their own experiences. The outcome from using a descriptive case is that students clearly understand how the situation described in the case can be analysed using the set of concepts provided. The purpose of a descriptive case is thus to illustrate concepts using a real-life example.

Evaluative Cases

An evaluative case (also called an evaluation case) is more complex than a descriptive case but less complex than a decision case. An evaluative case presents students with the facts of a situation and asks them to choose the theories or concepts that can explain or analyse the situation (Ellet, 2007; Naumes and Naumes, 2015). This kind of case is often used in undergraduate exams or assignments where students are presented with a description of a situation and then asked to provide their analysis of the situation by selecting the most applicable course concepts. Whereas in a descriptive case students know which concepts the case is meant to illustrate, an evaluative case leaves the selection open and tests students' ability to appropriately apply the most fitting concepts for the situation. The outcome from using an evaluative case is that students clearly understand which concepts are most appropriate to analyse the situation, why certain models are more applicable than others, and how to apply them properly to analyse the situation.

Rules Cases

When the case learning objectives relate to applying mathematical or technical rules in fields like finance, accounting, or statistics, these cases are sometimes called rules cases (Ellet, 2007; 2018). This is because they are intended to ensure students can translate the rules they have learned for a particular quantitative analysis to the described context. Rules-based cases can be descriptive where students are told which rules to apply, or evaluative if students must decide which rules they should apply in this situation. From using a rules case, students clearly see how to apply the rules they have learned and understand some of the challenges that can come up in real-world application such as judgement calls.

Critical Incident Cases

A critical incident case is an open-ended description of a challenging situation where students must decide how to act based on their own knowledge and background rather than on only included case data (Naumes and Naumes, 2015). They are typically quite short and include only limited background information. This type of case often relates to an unexpected crisis facing an organization where students debate the merits of different approaches in response to the crisis. While decision cases ask students to decide what the case protagonist should do based on the data in the case, a critical incident case asks students what *they* themselves would personally do if faced with the described situation based on their own life experience. Critical incident cases typically do not have solutions per se, but are intended to explore the pros and cons of various response options. Critical incident cases help students understand how their values, knowledge, and skills influence their choice of response compared to that of their classmates.

ALTERNATIVE CASE FORMATS

The following types of cases relate to different formats in which cases can be prepared and delivered. Please see Chapter 10 on special types of cases for more detail.

Short or Micro Cases

The term short case means a decision case using either primary or secondary data where the main case document must not exceed a maximum page length, typically three or four pages of text narrative and a limited number of pages of exhibits. Micro cases are even shorter, usually limited to two pages. Short cases have become much more popular recently as instructors believe that student willingness to read longer cases has declined. The rationale for short cases is that it is better to assign students a short case that they are more likely to read and therefore be able to learn from the class discussion than to assign them longer cases that they will not read, meaning that they will be unable to participate in and learn from the discussion. Case journals frequently have special calls for short cases, and many case outlets have placed upper page limits on case text and supporting exhibits. It is safe to say that the future of case research is short cases. That said, short cases typically do not have short accompanying IMs, so short case authors be forewarned. It is also particularly challenging to write a short case with all the relevant information to sustain a robust class discussion, given the decision case convention to exclude external research for the in-class case discussion.

Video Cases

Video cases present the case data in video format rather than – or in addition to – written format. A fully video case will cover the complete data set in visual form and students must complete the analysis solely based on what they discover in the video. Other video cases have both a written narrative case as well as an essential video component that is critical for the case analysis (see Sharen, 2016, for example). Video cases have become more common due to improvements in the ease of video creation and distribution for case authors. Also, the move to more video cases reflects the widely held belief among instructors that contemporary students would rather watch videos than read, and so are more likely to be prepared and learn from a video case than a traditional one. Although case publishers do occasionally have special issue calls for non-narrative cases, the vast majority of published cases are still written.

Multi-Media Cases

Multi-media cases are slightly different from pure video cases. While multi-media cases often include video interviews with individuals talking about the company or the decision, they also include a written case plus links to online resources and exhibits supporting the case, including elements such as financial data (e.g., balance sheets, income statements), store layouts and locations, organization charts, and marketing material. These types of cases are often hosted on a case publishing platform given the technology requirements to support the case. While very engaging and popular with students given their dynamic nature, they are the most complex case format for authors and only recommended for the most experienced case writers who also have technical acumen. For a splendid example of a multi-media case, see Gupta et al. (2015) *Eataly: Reimagining the Grocery Store* published by Harvard Business Publishing.

Graphic Cases

Graphic cases are pictorially depicted cases that are published in a form like a graphic novel. Like video cases, graphic cases have become more common due to improved ease of creation and distribution, as well as the perception that students are more likely to prepare and therefore learn from a non-narrative case. Although still uncommon in published case collections, graphic cases are becoming more widely recognized.

Virtual Cases

A virtual case is one written and designed for use in an online environment, with specific guidance in the IM/TN on how to use it in the online (often asynchronous) classroom. Most cases that are not designed for online use can still be used virtually with some preparation and a little modification. Some cases are particularly effective when used virtually, such as those where you do not want student views to be influenced by the others in the class. Whether a case is intended for online use or not, increasingly many publishers are now asking authors to address how the case could be used virtually in their IM/TNs.

Flipped Cases

While case analysis, by its nature, already incorporates many of the increasingly popular elements of flipped learning (Prud'homme-Généreux et al., 2017), traditional case analysis restricts students to only using the information provided in the case for their analysis. This has been done to mimic real world scenarios where decisions must be made with incomplete information. If a case is being used for evaluative purposes (e.g., midterm, final examination), it also ensures that students are doing their analysis with the same information, so any one student does not have an advantage over another. Flipped cases switch up this paradigm, providing less case narrative and fewer exhibits and requiring students to conduct external analysis to augment the information provided. This introduces more variability into the classroom discussion (given the multiplicity of information sources) and gives students practice in honing their research skills. The analysis for a flipped case can be done prior to the class discussion or as part of the class.

Live Cases

A live case is a specific type of primary source decision case where the focal case question is one the organization is still in the process of considering (i.e., it is still undecided), where the organization and students working on the case are able to interact with one another, and where the students are not limited only to the data included in the case description. Live cases are similar to student consulting projects, but are usually shorter in duration, smaller in scope, and begin with a predefined focal case question like a traditional decision case.

ADVANTAGES OF CASE WRITING

When you write and publish a case, plenty of people can benefit from being involved in the process: students; organizations; alumni; schools and programmes; and authors. Next, we will talk about the many reasons why a case research practice should be part of your scholarly work.

Students and Instructors

Students and instructors from around the world will be able to learn from you via your case and IM/TN. If you want to have impact in management education, this is one of the best ways to influence your field and those within it. The cases you write can help instructors teach students you will never meet. Students who have the good fortune of having their own instructor teach one of his or her cases in class know that it is a special experience to have a case taught by the case author. Teaching your own cases is also a lot of fun!

Case Organizations and Alumni

Writing cases is a fantastic way to engage with the organizations in your local community. Scholars can sometimes feel as if they are stuck on campus in their offices and become out of touch with what is going on in the broader business community. Writing cases is a way to build relationships with business leaders in your community. It is also a fantastic way to engage alumni with the school. Some of our most interesting cases have come from alumni of our institution who loved learning with cases and were eager to have us write a case on their organization to inspire the next generation of business students.

Business Schools and Programmes

Working with local organizations and alumni on cases is also a wonderful way to support your school's development office. We have worked with our development office to write cases on organizations who have financially contributed to the school, being careful to ensure that we have the latitude to create a robust, interesting, decision-focused case. It can also be helpful to your school's marketing or public relations efforts to show how faculty, students, and organizations are working together to enhance student learning. This is particularly true if the case connects with the school's research efforts as well. Programmes benefit from faculty case research because they often face gaps in pedagogy that are not easily filled. Cases that are written to fill programme gaps are especially helpful. Increasingly, case research is also a key factor in business school accreditation processes.

Authors and Publishers

Publishers of course benefit when authors publish cases with them, which is why they typically pay a small royalty based on case sales. While you will not get rich publishing cases, royalty cheques can be substantial on best-selling cases. More than money though, case research can help build your reputation and credibility as a scholar, especially since case writing is a skill set in which many scholars are not trained. As case publishers become more selective in the cases they publish, the value of case research is growing with respect to case publications counting towards hiring and tenure decisions. This is especially true with the rise of professional teaching positions where case publications are often valued. Case research can be a way to build your reputation and relationships in the business community. Those connections can help you figure out how to translate some of your other research into educational usage, and to help keep you abreast of practice changes in your field of expertise. As an instructor, writing a case can be a solution to a gap in your syllabus for which you have never been able to find the right case. Using your own cases in your classrooms can be a lot of fun for everyone and one of the best learning opportunities for your students. Because it is a quite different focus from other forms of research, case research can be a way to make progress on your scholarly goals while other projects are stuck or on hold. Finally, as we have said before, case research is one of the most effective ways to have impact in management education because of students and instructors all over the world learning from your cases.

Figure 1.1   Who benefits from case writing?

STEPS TO WRITING A CASE

The rest of this book is devoted to the many steps in the process of writing and publishing a case. In Chapter 2 we will explore what makes for an interesting case so we can consider those characteristics in our decision-making. Chapter 3 is devoted to determining the type of case you wish to write and understanding the consequences of those choices. Chapter 4 outlines how to get started writing your case. In Chapter 5 we will focus on how to research primary data cases, while in Chapter 6 we will examine how to research secondary data cases. Chapter 7 describes the case writing and revising process. Chapter 8 outlines the process of creating a teaching note or an instructor's manual. Chapter 9 explains how to test your case prior to submission to a publisher. Chapter 10 discusses special case formats such as short cases, video and multi-media cases, graphic cases, flipped cases, student written cases, live cases, virtual cases, and audio/podcast cases. Chapter 11 explains how to get your case published. Chapter 12 covers our last words on the art of writing cases and conducting case research. Finally, we provide an Appendix at the end that outlines key resources on case research for those who would like more information.

KEY CHAPTER TAKEAWAYS

• Writing and publishing business cases – or a case research practice – is one of the most effective ways of being an impactful management scholar.
• A decision-based case is the most common type, which is a pedagogical tool based on primary or secondary data that outlines a factual issue, challenge or opportunity facing an organization where the case protagonist must decide on a course of action. Other case types include descriptive, evaluative, rules, critical incident, and hypothetical. Most cases are written in narrative long form, but other forms include short, video, multi-media, graphic, virtual, flipped, live, and audio/podcast.
• The case method builds analytical, critical thinking, communication, and problem-solving skills through active participation. There are many advantages to case writing and publishing for authors, students, instructors, organizations, alumni, schools, and programmes.
• The steps to writing and publishing cases including instructor's manuals (IM), or teaching notes (TN) are covered in the following chapters.

We hope you are excited to learn more about case research. Next, we discuss all the factors that make for an interesting case so you can soon get started on writing your own.

NOTE

1.   The terms instructor's manual (IM) and teaching note (TN) are largely inter-
      changeable, with each publication outlet preferring one or the other. Check the
      publisher's website for the appropriate term as well as required contents and
      format. For brevity, throughout this book we refer to this document as the IM/
      TN.

2. What makes a case interesting?

Publishing a case is a lot of work. As a scholar, it is also a fantastic way to make an impact in your field. You want your case to have the biggest impact it can, which means it has to appeal to both students and instructors as well as publishers. In later chapters, we will review how you can best refine your case and instructor's manual or teaching note (IM/TN) by classroom testing them (Chapter 9) and how best to prepare your case for publication (Chapter 11). What we will discuss in this chapter are the upfront choices you can make early on to ensure your case is as interesting and appealing as possible. First, we outline the characteristics with respect to topic choice, followed by writing style factors, and finally the teaching or IM/TN components that all work together to build a winning case. If you find a great topic and do a terrific job writing the case and IM/TN, you could find yourself as a best-selling case author.

There are three main upfront areas of consideration for authors when thinking about the factors that make a case interesting for students and instructors. The first set relates to the topic choices an author makes about the subject of the case. This includes the choice of focal firm, the time period of the case, the identity of the case protagonist, the key case question, and the main theoretical, conceptual, and research concepts the case is intended to explore. The second set relates to the writing choices an author makes when communicating the case story. This includes choices about how to start the case, how to describe the main decision point, what data to include in the case, and how best to format the case. The third set relates to the early choices an author makes about how to teach the case, including any interesting presentations, questions, analyses, or perspectives.

TOPIC CHOICES

The choices you make as an author about the case topic are arguably the most influential in terms of making your case interesting. The topics you choose to focus on are like the foundation of your case, and if you lay a strong foundation, you are more likely to successfully write and teach a great case. This section outlines the factors to consider when choosing case topics that will influence how interesting students and instructors will find the case. Remember that at the end of the day, an author's enthusiasm for a topic comes through to readers, so it always helps to choose a topic that you are interested in and then do your best to convince users that you are right. Nevertheless, there are some predictable patterns which excite and interest case readers. There are also ways you can construct a case to make it fun for an instructor to teach. If you want to maximize your chance of writing a case that will be interesting to lots of people, consider the factors outlined below in your topic choices. Note that not every case has to have all of these elements, but cases that have several of these characteristics are more likely to be well received by students and instructors.

Well-known Organization

One of the best ways to generate interest in your case right from the start is to choose a well-known organization as the subject of the case. When case users, both students and instructors, see a case about an organization they know, the case is immediately more accessible and appealing to them because they already understand quite a bit about the context in which the case occurs. For instance, when students know the case company from the case title, they probably already understand the industry in which the firm competes, the products it sells, the business model it uses, the countries in which the firm operates, who their main competitors are, and possibly even who the senior leaders are in the organization. Think of a company like Tesla, Inc. (Tesla). There have been a number of cases written on Tesla over the years which have been wildly popular with students. Before students even read the case, they are often familiar with the core product (cars), the industry (electric vehicles), the geography (increasingly global), and the CEO (Elon Musk). Students are eager to read the case and come into class for the linked analysis, be it marketing, operations, strategy, or organizational behaviour. This familiarity gives case users a big leg up in understanding the case and helps students build self-efficacy with respect to their ability to crack the case.

If you look at the lists of best-selling cases at the major publishing houses, they almost always include cases on big international firms that everybody knows. Of course, they are often also market-leading firms with a huge influence in their industries, and so they are rightfully important for students to study and understand. For all of these reasons, many case writers want to write cases about well-known firms, although such firms can be difficult to gain access to in order to gather primary data unless one happens to have a good contact. Even if one has a good contact, there are often far more hurdles in terms of internal approvals for the eventual release and publication of such a case. Hence, many case writers choose to write secondary source cases about such firms, which is usually possible if the company is public since plenty of data are available (see Schnarr and Rowe, 2014).

Keep in mind, though, that while case users tend to love cases about firms they already know, reading a case about a cool, new, up-and-coming firm can also be interesting for students. In that case, the case writer has to work harder to introduce the firm properly so readers understand it well enough to conduct a solid analysis. Lastly, cases that are locally situated can also be interesting to users because the organizations are known in the region but do not have broad exposure (see Schnarr et al., 2016 about a local hockey club, or Woodwark et al., 2020b about a regional convenience store chain).

While using a well-known company may seem a superficial way to approach case writing, do not underestimate the importance of the increasing challenge with student engagement. As we will discuss in Chapter 10 when we look at alternative case formats including short cases and multi-media cases, instructors can make their lives easier by meeting students halfway and using cases that involve known companies operating in cool industries facing interesting challenges. To provide instructors with that opportunity requires a case catalogue that includes such cases, which provides a fantastic opportunity for case writers! A good trick to start is to think of a well-known company with interesting challenges, and then do a quick search of the case catalogues of case publishers such as Ivey Publishing or Harvard Business Publishing to see if there is already a recently published case on that company in the area in which you are intending to focus. If there is, you may want to start your search for a new case company again. If not, you may wish to check with your target publisher to ensure they do not already have a case on that company in the publishing pipeline before you put a lot of work into a case that will soon be scooped. Some publishers will let you know in advance whether your proposed case is about the same issue as an in-press case on the same company. It never hurts to ask case publishers in advance to let you know if your proposed new case might be attractive to them. In our experience, the worst thing that can happen is that you do not get a response, but typically publishers would rather redirect authors to another case than to receive duplicate submissions.

Sexy Industry

Let's face it; some industries are simply sexier than others. For instance, technology company cases will reliably glean more student interest than utility cases. Firms that are in new industries or disrupting existing industries are also more interesting than firms with stable on-going operations. Sexy industries like technology also tend to get more media coverage, so students are more likely to be familiar with companies in that space. Often students own or use the technology products being discussed. Some industries, such as entertainment (e.g., movies/streaming services, video games, and theme parks), are inherently interesting to a broad range of people, while other industries, such as financial services, tend to appeal to a smaller segment. It is worth remembering, though, that unusual industries can also be interesting by virtue of their novelty and uniqueness (see Schnarr et al., 2021 about a ballet; and Woodwark and Wong, 2013 about a luthier). To get you started, popular industries can include those such as airlines, artificial intelligence/machine learning, automotive, cryptocurrency, fintech, grocery, sports, fashion, restaurants, luxury brands, virtual reality, and wineries/breweries.

Recent Timing

Cases can get stale-dated quickly and old cases have unique challenges to teaching effectively. Although there are classic cases that defy the rules (see Berg and Fast, 1975), in general recent cases are more interesting and relatable than older cases. This is especially true if the firm or industry has had recent media coverage or if their business model has significantly changed over the years. As an example, current undergraduate students are not likely to remember that Netflix started out as a company that mailed customers up to three DVDs at a time. Customers would watch the DVDs at their leisure and then mail them back to Netflix to receive the next movies on their list. Of course, that was disrupted by Netflix becoming a streaming service. It is challenging to teach a Netflix case focused on their old delivery model to students who have only experienced their current streaming format. For instructors, recent cases are an easy sell to students whereas older cases can be an uphill battle to explain their ongoing relevance. A case set more than three years ago also increases the risk that students will just check online to see what the company did and how it worked out. Finally, if the ultimate goal is publication, that process can sometimes take over a year or more, which will draw out the focal time of the case even further. Some publishing outlets will not accept cases when the time of the case is more than eight years in the past. A possible solution to a number of these challenges is writing a case ripped from recent headlines; this can be a great way to bring immediate organizational issues into your classroom.

Clear Controversy or Tension

Recall that the purpose of a case is to respectfully debate different perspectives and arrive on a recommended course of action given the available evidence. Cases that have a clear tension or apparent controversy are more interesting for users because there is a solid argument on both or multiple sides. Cases with only two possible sides that are mutually exclusive – such as yes/no or go/no-go decisions – can be especially fun in class because participants are necessarily in one camp or the other (see Casciaro et al., 2005a about whether employees of a mattress firm should do a ropes course). Tension in cases reflects what happens in workplaces and highlights to students that they will not be allowed to 'fence-sit' when called upon to weigh in on proposed decisions in their future roles. It is also a key element of what case journals and case publishers are looking for in the cases they accept.

Relatable Protagonist

The protagonist in a case is the key decision-maker to whom students are introduced through the case data. While some cases are written without a protagonist, these are less engaging for readers as the story element of the case is less compelling. Think of reading a book where it is just a description of events with no characters to introduce dynamism into the story. Having a relatable protagonist (along with other voices in the case to create the tension noted above) can really make your case come alive, particularly when students see themselves represented. It is worth noting that most case publishers prefer a single, main protagonist with secondary, supporting voices to add additional insight to the narrative.

It is very important to point out that over the past decade, case writers and publishers have come under fire for a lack of protagonist diversity in case collections, especially due to the lack of female or racialized protagonists in cases and because of biased portrayals of diverse protagonists such as the gendered representation of female protagonists in published cases (Grandy and Ingols, 2016; Sharen and McGowan, 2019). Given the diversity of students in contemporary business schools, it is important for students to be exposed to a diverse range of protagonists in terms of gender, ethnicity, age, backgrounds, and geography. Many case publishers, authors, and reviewers are now working to build a more diverse set of protagonists in our case collections so that more students are able to see more of themselves represented in their classrooms. When students can relate to case protagonists in a personal way – especially if they have had few prior chances to do so – it is particularly engaging. For recommendations about how you can make your cases more diversity friendly, see Woodwark and Grandy (2022).

Relatable Focal Issue

Focal case issues to which students can relate make for interesting cases, particularly when students have had to deal with similar issues themselves or can easily understand being in that position. Such cases often have to do with almost universal topics like money, career negotiations, or managing the boss. One of our favourite human resource management cases discusses an organization that is unable to provide wage increases again and suggests how to address the consequences of that fact (see MacMillan, 2011). As consumers, students can relate to cases where businesses are losing market share or when new competition is entering the industry. Similar to cases where students are familiar with the company or industry, decision cases with a relatable focus make the case more interesting to read, analyse, and subsequently discuss in class.

Issues that Matter to Students

Firms – and therefore cases about firms – do not exist in a vacuum. Firms exist within a broader community and have important impacts on their community's economic well-being as well as the area's social and environmental well-being. Many students are very interested in the broader social discussions about important issues like climate change, social justice, or political movements such as the fight for democracy around the world. Cases that allow students to explore these kinds of issues from the perspective of a specific firm in a business context are interesting for students. Recognize that not every case has to have a focal case question about corporate social responsibility; rather, authors can choose to incorporate background data about how the firm manages these issues and students can explore whether or how that approach impacts the focal case decision.

Balanced Presentation

One thing that can turn students off a case is when it is overly positive and comes across as a commercial for the firm. No firm is perfect, and most firms have downsides and valid criticisms that should be reflected in the case to some extent. Including negative or less than positive information in a primary source case can be challenging because the author needs the company's sign-off and the company wants to look as good as possible. However, it is important to be balanced, especially if students are likely to be aware of unflattering firm information. In order to buy into the case analysis process, students need to know that the case is a fair representation of the firm and its focal decision. Hence, sometimes authors need to be creative in finding ways to incorporate fair criticism into their primary source cases so that the case author does not come across as biased towards or too soft on the firm. One way to include less than flattering (but truthful) information is to use secondary source media coverage to supplement the primary case data. Authors may also need to explain to their firm contacts why it is important for a case to appear balanced in its presentation, particularly when not including publicly known data will hurt the credibility of the case.

High Stakes

The more important the focal question is to the firm, the more interesting it is to students. Cases that ask students how to save firms from bankruptcy or hostile takeovers have clear high stakes for firms and students find such situations engaging. Similarly, decisions about whether or not to make a risky big bet – such as pivoting to another industry, region, or product – are interesting because if they get it wrong the downside is huge for the company.

Unexpected Perspectives

Cases can be interesting for users when they ask them to take perspectives they have never or rarely considered. A great way to get student attention is to flip the traditional perspective on its head. For instance, many cases ask students to consider the topic of gender and leadership from a female perspective, particularly in relation to family-to-work and work-to-family conflict. One of our favourite cases in organizational behaviour flips that expected dynamics on its head and asks students to consider family-to-work and work-to-family conflict from the perspective of working dads (see Konrad and Phillips, 2014). Shifting perspectives on familiar topics can bring interesting new insights that shed new light on old topics that might not otherwise be uncovered.

WRITING CHOICES

As an author, once you've made many of the topic choices that will help make your case interesting, your next challenge is to write it in a way that ensures its interest potential is realized. These are the writing style factors you should consider as an author when writing up your work for maximum impact.

Short Length

One of the biggest changes in case writing in the past decade is the move towards shorter cases. Cases that were 20 pages (or more) used to be common; most publishers now discourage cases over 10 pages (or even eight pages) of narrative and suggest that the sweet spot for a regular length case is about six pages with a few extra pages of exhibits, with strategic management cases often slightly longer at eight pages of text. Other case publishers request cases be no more than 2000 to 2500 words. The impetus for this trend to shorter cases seems to be the belief that contemporary students do not read long cases. Hence, instructors are reluctant to assign long cases and much prefer to assign short ones that they hope students will actually read. Instructors directly impact case sales through their case selection, and so many publishers no longer want

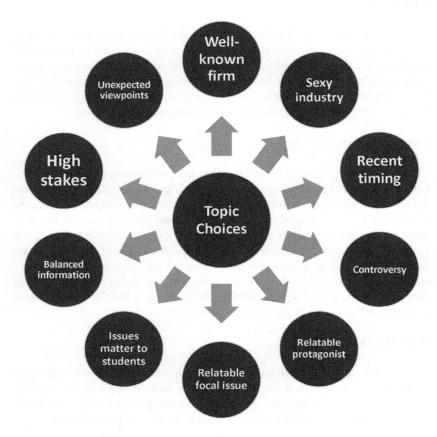

Figure 2.1   What topic choices make a case interesting?

to publish long cases that instructors will not adopt. Shorter cases for the most part sell better than long ones – unless the long ones are old classics or on extremely popular companies. Just as instructor preference for cases with an accompanying IM/TN made it a requirement to also publish them with each case, instructor preference for short cases is forcing case writers to keep cases short. This is resulting in higher demand for short cases, which is changing how cases are written. In a subsequent chapter, we will discuss this scenario in more detail, specifically referencing a trend by case journals to issue frequent calls for issues focused on very short cases, usually of no more than three or four pages. Regardless of the actual limit, the constraint on length means that authors have to be very focused in their writing and data presentation. It is important to note that just because a case may be short, case publishers will still require a robust IM/TN. Short cases often require longer IM/TNs to make sure that all of the necessary theory, resources, and analysis are there to make the case successful in the classroom.

Well-written

Cases should be tightly written and focus on data that is relevant to the focal case question. Authors and sometimes companies often want to include a lot of background data on the company or industry that is not directly relevant to the case question or analysis. Case writers need to be judicious and sparing in their writing, so ensure all the relevant case data required for the analysis is contained in the case and clearly communicated; this has become more challenging as case length has shrunk. One of the most traditional writing conventions for cases is that they are always written in the past tense, even if the situation being described is in fact on-going; the only exception within the case is for direct quotations which are used as stated. A best practice is to write the case and IM/TN almost concurrently, to ensure that all case questions actually are answerable with the data in the case. Any data in the case that is not used in the IM/TN for case analysis should be dropped. The writing process is very iterative; accept that your case will need to be revised and edited several times and is a living document until published. Before a case is even submitted to a publication outlet, the case will need to be revised after the IM/TN is complete, again after it is reviewed by a trusted colleague, and yet again after it has been tested in a classroom. A good rule of thumb is to stick to shorter paragraphs and sentences whenever possible. To get a sense about what is a well-written case, look at the best-selling case list through case publishers like Ivey Publishing. In addition to case examples we have previously mentioned, some of our favourites include Dolansky (2019), Boroff and Pratt (2017), and Myrah et al. (2021).

A well-written case is much more likely to be received favourably by reviewers and editors to move towards publication. Well-written cases are also more likely to be adopted by instructors and used by students. If you want all your work to be put to good use, make sure you invest sufficient time in writing your case and consider a professional editor to polish your work.

Strong Hooks and Action Triggers

The hook in a case is the introductory statement intended to grab the reader's attention and get them interested in reading the rest of the case. Often the hook is in the form of a question the protagonist is asking him or herself, or in the form of a quotation from them. There are lots of ways to create effective hooks, but the main idea is that the hook should pique the readers' interest and leave them wanting to learn more. In this way, case writing is very similar to story-telling; authors must make a compelling enough introduction that readers want to know more. Newspapers do this all of the time by making sure the intro-ductory paragraph provides enough context about what is going on (where, who, and when) and hints at the tension or conflict to come. Although brief, a good hook and introductory paragraph give readers a clear idea of what the case focus will be even if they do not yet fully understand the issues or context.

The action trigger in a case is the reason why the protagonist must decide now rather than later. Often the action trigger is an event that requires a response, or an upcoming event such as a meeting, a vote, or a deadline. The action trigger also helps to set the time frame of the case so that readers understand what time it is when the protagonist is deliberating. For instance, if the action trigger is an upcoming meeting this Tuesday, the reader needs to know what day and time it is now so they know how much time is left before the decision must be made. The time context is also important as it grounds the case in a particular moment which is linked to the subsequent analysis. For example, if a case is set in the early 2000s (which we would not recommend for the reasons outlined earlier), you would not expect students to suggest market-ing campaigns involving social media because it was not in existence. Cases in the North American grocery industry from, say, 2010 should not involve student analysis that suggests an online delivery channel because it was not a prevalent consumer modality at the time (and while increasing, in most of the world it is still much less than traditional grocery shopping).

A good case introductory paragraph(s) will include the case hook, the action trigger for the protagonist, and an initial description of the focal case question or decision point. It will let you know the company or industry, give you the geographic setting, and, as noted above, the time context. Case conferences that accept embryonic cases typically ask for the introductory paragraph(s) to use as the basis for discussion about a case in development. Great introductory paragraphs create excitement from the reader, but importantly, it is often what faculty read when deciding what cases to add to their course roster.

Clear Decision

In addition to the hook and action trigger, a good case introduction in deci-sion cases includes a clear description of the decision that must be made. For students to conduct an effective case analysis and advocate for one course of action over another, they must understand exactly the decision the protagonist needs to make and the primary alternatives. Excellent case introductions will make the focal decision clear upfront, and then authors typically reiterate the (same) main decision point near the end of the case once all the case data has been presented. This technique brings the decision to the reader's mind early on, so they have that context as they read through the rest of the case. By ensuring the question is clear again at the end, it further cements the decision focus in the mind of the reader as they launch into the case analysis. Be sure that each time you phrase the case decision it is actually asking the same question and not a slightly different (or new) question. As experienced case writers know, it is much more difficult than expected to articulate a clear decision question. The best way to ensure readers correctly understand the case question is to conduct an in-class testing of the case (see Chapter 9).

Sufficient Data for Analysis

One of the most challenging elements of writing a great case is making sure that your case includes all the data students require to thoroughly answer the discussion questions suggested in the IM/TN. If the information is not contained in the case itself, you cannot assume that students will be aware of it, and traditional case analysis assumes that students are not allowed to use external data sources to support their case analysis. So, everything students will need to know to analyse the case must be in the case narrative or exhibits. Given that authors typically know much more about the company and issue than what ends up being included, compounded by the fact that authors are under pressure to keep cases short, ensuring all the required data is in the case is trickier than it might seem. Case reviewers and editors typically pay a lot of attention to whether the IM/TN uses any data for analysis that is not in the case. Making sure this alignment exists between the case and the IM/TN is another reason why testing your case is so important.

Clear Format and Headings

Following a typical case format that includes all the expected sections helps students understand the case as they read through it. As this can be idiosyncratic to the business discipline, a good idea is to model your case format after a few of your own personal favourite cases from your topic area (see Chapter 12 for additional insight on this point). While cases have very few hard and fast rules about format, there needs to be a logical flow to the presentation of information, creating a path that readers are able to follow easily. Making good use of headings helps readers visualize the organization of the case data and enhances readability by visually breaking up the page.

Supporting Materials

Supporting materials such as data files, simulation exercises, and videos can help make cases more interactive and therefore more interesting for students. Data files can be particularly helpful if you are publishing cases in accounting, finance, analytics, or operations. Most publishers will support your request to include supporting materials with your case, but do discuss this with them as soon as possible, particularly if the use of the supporting materials is required to follow the suggested teaching approach outlined in your IM/TN. You also should check to make sure that their publishing house has the capability to host the supporting materials; materials such as data files in Excel are usually not a problem but not all publishers have the ability to host simulations or videos. Public supporting materials can be used as well, although recognize that they may not always be available and often require you to gain permission from the source of the materials if you want them to be included with your case.

Disguises

While somewhat counter-intuitive, disguising the company can sometimes make a case more interesting to students because it can be a lot of fun to speculate and argue about which firm it could be. Disguises are sometimes used because firms do not want to have their name clearly associated with the case facts, in which case a disguise allows authors to publish despite these concerns. With that kind of disguise, authors cannot reveal the actual firm name in the IM/TN. However, with the firm's permission, authors can use disguises upfront and then allow instructors to reveal the true identity in class as part of the case analysis or epilogue (see Brittain and Sitkin, 2008; Lakshminarayanan and Hanspal, 2014). The disguised components can include changing the name of the firm, the names of the people involved, often changing the geographic location of the case, and firm size. Making the focal firm a mystery can help prevent students from leaning too heavily on their preconceptions about the firm, issue, or people involved. Disguised cases make great exam cases because students are not able to search the company online to find out what they may have done. The downside to writing a disguised cases is that they are sometimes more difficult to get published.

It is important to distinguish between fully disguised cases and disguising data in cases. Often data is disguised in otherwise public cases to protect confidential or proprietary information such as product margins, market share, or financial performance. This is different from fully disguised cases where the context and decision is the same, and often the industry does not change but the rest of the information is shifted to protect the anonymity of the organization. Fully disguised cases are also different from hypothetical cases. In the former, it is a real company where the decision being considered actually happened. In hypothetical cases, the situation did not actually happen and was constructed for students to work through the scenario.

IM/TEACHING CHOICES

Case authors can also help make cases interesting for users by having creative and challenging teaching approaches outlined in their IM/TN. In this scenario, student interest is piqued by how the case is conducted in class; ideally this is more dynamic than just having the students respond to the analysis questions posed in the IM/TN. These are factors that authors can consider when outlining their suggested teaching approach in the IM/TN to help engage students.

Novel Way to Introduce, Present, or Analyse Case

A great way to make your case interesting to students is to design it with an unusual introduction, a novel presentation, or a thought-provoking new analytical approach. For instance, we have started the historic case *Cola Wars Continue: Coke and Pepsi in 2010* by David Yoffe and Renee Kim (2011) by showing historic soft drink ads over the years demonstrating how they evolve, and by conducting the Pepsi Challenge taste test in class. The internet makes company information, especially videos, very accessible, which is a great way to kick off a class and a good resource to include in IM/TNs. Disguises and twists in presentation – or even deception – can also be effective in getting students' attention and interest. An example of this kind of approach is Colleen Sharen's (2016) case with accompanying videos called *The Balancing Act: Making Tough Decisions.* After reading that case, students are asked to watch a video of the protagonist and evaluate his/her leadership effectiveness. The catch is that there are four different portrayals of the protagonist speaking the same script but with actors varying by gender and race. After an initial discussion about the focal decision and the protagonist, the instructor can reveal that different students were shown different videos, only one of which is the actual protagonist. Hence, a case that initially appears to be about only a change management process at a non-profit, leads to an additional discussion about leadership, gender, and race. The element of surprise is very effective in making a case interesting and memorable.

Questions that Challenge Students

Challenging case questions are a must for capturing student interest. Case assignment questions that are too easy or only ask students to reiterate case facts are not motivating. Ensure your assignment questions challenge students to make tough decisions and to defend their rationales. Assignment questions are an opportunity for students to apply critical thinking to the data that is presented in the case. In addition, case questions that students have been asked to prepare in advance can make for great debate fodder. Changing the format for reviewing student answers from large class discussion to debate format, for instance, can make the analysis process varied, dynamic, and challenging for students and can also include students who might not otherwise volunteer to participate.

Counter-intuitive Analysis or Conclusions

Cases that challenge the way students think about things – including the assumptions they may not know they hold – or challenge what they think they already know, are a sure way to capture student attention. Kirk Hanson and Stephen Weiss's (1991) multi-staged case on the development of a cure for river blindness at Merck & Co. called *Merck & Co., Inc.: Addressing Third-World Needs* leads students through a series of increasingly escalating scenarios that seem to contradict expected business practices. It is also a great example of a case with clear tension and conflict. Cases that showcase the exception to accepted rules always make for interesting discussions in class.

Making the Discussion Inclusive

Finally, cases are interesting to students when they can express themselves and see elements of themselves represented. This can be accomplished by including multiple voices and perspectives in the case. Be sure to consider a broad range of perspectives in your case and IM/TN preparation. For more on inclusive cases, see Woodwark and Grandy (2022).

KEY CHAPTER TAKEAWAYS

- Your topic choices, writing choices, and IM/TN teaching choices are all factors that influence how interesting students and instructors will find your case.
- When choosing your case topic, consider factors such as a well-known organization, a sexy industry, recent timing, clear controversy or tension, a relatable protagonist, a relatable focal issue, issues that matter to students, balanced presentation, high stakes, and unexpected perspectives.
- In writing up your case, consider keeping the case short, ensure it is well-written, include strong hooks and action triggers, write a clear decision to be made, ensure there is sufficient data for the analysis, use a clear

format with headings, provide relevant supporting materials, and consider a disguise if it makes sense for your case.

- When designing your IM/TN and teaching approach, ensure you incorporate novel ways you can present your case, challenging case questions, any counter-intuitive conclusions, and how you can make the case discussion inclusive for all students.
- Devoting time upfront to ensuring your case is as interesting as possible is well worth it. Your choice and framing of the topic, how you write or otherwise present your case, and how you design it for teaching can all influence the positive reception your case receives and ultimately its readership.

Next, we will talk about how to determine the type of case you wish to write.

3. Determining the type of case to write

When you decide to write a case, one of the first steps in the process is to determine what type of case you are going to write. Earlier chapters have discussed the various types of cases that can be written. We are assuming that if you are reading this book, you are primarily interested in this most common case type – the decision- or problem-based case. This case type is by far the most commonly published type of case in most disciplines. Most authors have this format as an objective when they start to write a case. This chapter will focus on the other key decisions that you are going to need to make before you start writing your case and instructor's manual or teaching note (IM/TN).

There are multiple decisions to make along the journey of developing a case including whether you are going to write this case by yourself or with one or several co-authors, the disciplinary perspective (e.g., marketing, accounting, operations, etc.) from which you will be analysing the case, the main theory or analysis tool on which you want the case to focus, the intended level of students (e.g., undergraduate, graduate, executive, etc.), the position in the course (e.g., at the beginning where it is more of an introduction to concepts or at the end where it is a more mature consideration of concepts), and what type of data source you wish to use, namely primary or secondary. Some of these factors will be choices you have to make, while others will be determined by the constraints you face with respect to the particular case you want to write, especially due to data availability. Likewise, some of these factors will be evident from the beginning of your process, while others may have to be decided or even changed as you work through the process. At the end of the day, each case evolves as a result of the decisions the case author(s) makes combined with the opportunities and limitations they encounter in the process. Sometimes the case you initially wanted to write is not possible, but in our experience if authors are flexible and open to new directions, there is usually a way to write a great albeit different case than you initially envisioned. The more experience you get in writing different kinds of cases, the better you will be able to anticipate issues upfront and design around them.

CASES AND TENURE

For those of you on the tenure-track stream at your institution, a special note about case writing and tenure. Before you commit time to case writing, ensure you fully understand whether and how your institution counts case research and publication in its tenure process. Some schools are delighted to see pre-tenure faculty working on cases and will view case conference presentations and case submissions or publications very favourably. Other schools discourage their pre-tenure faculty from doing any case writing until post-tenure, if ever. Make sure you really understand what the incentives and disincentives are at your school before you devote precious time and energy on case writing. While case writing is fun, challenging, and impactful, your best bet may be to wait until post-tenure if your institution does not count case writing towards meeting tenure research requirements. With the rise of Professional Teaching Positions or Teaching Stream tenure-track positions, whether or not case writing counts for tenure may also vary by the type of position you hold. The bottom line is that you should be clear about how case writing is evaluated at your institution before you start a pre-tenure case writing practice.

WHAT IS YOUR GOAL OF WRITING A CASE?

Arguably the most important decision when you begin to write a case is to identify your core goal. It is a very different commitment to write a case for publication in a top-tier peer-reviewed case journal than it is to write a case for use in your class, or for development at a case conference. We strongly recommend being clear from the start about your goal for the case you are working on so you understand the full extent of what will be required to be successful. Ideally, we recommend matching your goal level to your case writing experience level by setting easier goals initially and then building to more challenging goals as you gain experience. We outline below what we think are appropriate beginner, intermediate, and advanced case writer goals. These goal difficulty levels are driven in part by the amount of time authors should expect it will take them to achieve, so be sure to consider when you want or need your case work to be completed when you decide which goal level to choose. Realistically, having a case accepted in a top-tier, peer-review case journal such as the *Case Review Journal* can take well over a year or more as it goes through the creation, testing (in a classroom and through a case conference), journal submission, and review process.

Beginner Goals

Appropriate beginner level goals include:

- drafting a new case that you can test and use in your own classroom;
- writing a draft case introduction and outline for a conference embryo[1] (or cases in development) case track; and,

- drafting a hypothetical case to learn the proper case form.

These beginner goals represent minimal upfront effort but can provide feedback to authors quickly about the potential the case has for future development. Authors can then choose whether to increase their goal for that case to an intermediate one if they feel the case has further potential. Note that it is a typically acceptable practice at most case conferences with an embryo track to present the case in the embryo track one year and then present the fully developed case at the full case track the following year, or to submit the developed full case to the associated journal following the conference. The purpose of such tracks is to help authors develop their cases into viable full cases for later consideration to present or publish. Embryo cases typically do not require company sign-off as they represent initial thoughts or ideas from which a full case could develop. These beginner goals can all be accomplished in a short period of time such as one or two months.

Intermediate Goals

Intermediate level goals would include:

- testing your draft case in someone else's classroom;
- preparing a full case for use in a student case competition;
- submitting a full case to a case conference in the appropriate disciplinary track; and,
- submitting a full case to a non-peer-reviewed publication such as a textbook.

Intermediate goals require the development of a full case and IM/TN, and ideally allow authors to get more feedback about the effectiveness of their case without committing to a lengthy peer-review process. There are a number of international student case competitions that put out a call for cases that have not been published for use during the competition (this is discussed more in Chapters 9 and 11). Some of these calls are an opportunity to write and test out a case with a broad audience as part of the case competition and can be a bit faster to write as they do not always require an accompanying IM/TN. There is sometimes a publication opportunity for cases selected for the case competition with publishing houses that have partnered with the case competition organization. Full peer-reviewed conferences with a case track(s) do usually require a fully developed IM/TN and also require sign-off from the company if the case has been written using primary data sources. Typically, submissions to conferences with case tracks that are peer reviewed will receive reviewer feedback to help authors improve their work prior to presentation at the conference, but authors are not required to complete all the suggestions before the conference. However, it is a wonderful opportunity to improve the draft case prior to the conference so that authors can receive further feedback during the conference on a more developed version of the case and IM/TN. Intermediate level goals are all achievable within one term or quarter.

Advanced Goals

Advanced level goals would include:

- submitting a full case for review to a competitive case publisher like Ivey Publishing, or the Case Centre; and,
- submitting a full case for review at a peer-reviewed case journal like the *Case Research Journal* or *The CASE Journal*.

At the advanced and most challenging level, authors will need a well-polished case and IM/TN, sign-off from the case company (again, if it is based on primary data), and sufficient time to commit to rounds of revisions requested by either reviewers or editors. Advanced goals like these may take as little as half a year for a case with few revisions or may take multiple years to success-fully publish after several rounds of revisions.

SOLO OR CO-AUTHORS

An important decision to make early on is whether to write your case alone or with a co-author or co-authors. In part, this decision depends on whether you have potential co-authors who share your goals for the case. Although it can be satisfying to write your case solo since you get all the credit (and all of the royalties if published), there are plenty of benefits to working with a co-author, particularly if you are new to case writing. A co-author can help with all aspects of the case and can help reduce the workload that each person must complete. They can also bring new perspectives and knowledge to the case including expertise in other disciplines, which can be important in developing your case to its fullest potential. Co-authors can also round out skills in areas where you have less experience; in general, less experienced case authors are wise to partner with more experienced ones as they learn the process. An experienced co-author can save a novice a lot of time and effort by directing the case development with detailed feedback and advice. Co-authors can also be helpful in testing cases, developing IM/TNs, and responding to reviewers, so sometimes additional authors are brought on to a case for that purpose (e.g., Rowe et al., 2011). Most published cases these days tend to be co-authored, which we think speaks to the wisdom of that strategy, especially considering most authors will receive almost the same credit (although fewer royalties) for co-authored cases as for solo cases. Overall, there are plenty of great reasons to co-author your cases. If you are a doctoral or a master's student, you may need to add your thesis advisor or a faculty member to your case as some publishers will only accept cases with a recognized faculty member as one of the authors.

The only major downside is the risk of co-author conflict and its negative impact on the quality of the work as well as your enjoyment of the experience. Choose your co-authors with care, clearly establish who has the responsibility as lead author, and be prepared to leave the project if necessary. Remember that if you initially proceed as a solo author, you can always add a co-author later if you find you need additional expertise to meet your goal. In particular, if you are responding to reviewers' or editors' comments at a peer-reviewed journal, you may find the direction in which they are asking you to take your case is beyond your expertise. Bringing in a co-author to fill in the gaps at that point is still an option even if you started the process solo. Just be clear about roles and expectations when adding authors to your cases.

DISCIPLINE

Most of us will primarily write cases in our own main disciplines because it is what we are most familiar and comfortable with. For example, our fields are strategic management and organizational behaviour so most of our cases are in our own areas. However, we have both had the opportunity to work on cases outside our disciplines, including in marketing and entrepreneurship, as well as interdisciplinary area like healthcare management and not-for-profit management. With few exceptions about how cases are used in specific disciplines (e.g., accounting or finance classes using rules-based cases), the case writing process is often very similar across disciplines. Hence, experienced case writers can typically work across disciplines provided they have a co-author who can guide the development of the IM/TN, which is the most discipline-specific part of the case. Before you work on cases outside of your discipline, particularly pre-tenure, ensure your institution recognizes such work outside your main discipline. This question can come up during the peer-review process where editors and reviewers can recommend that a case you have framed as a strategy case would be better positioned as a marketing case. A switch in discipline can also happen with a secondary source case where the publicly available data are simply not available for the case you initially expected to write, but the case can be done if the primary focus shifts. Be open to possible shifts in case discipline compared to what you intended. This could involve a change in the level of analysis; organizational behaviour cases often focus at the individual or team level, while strategic management cases will have a company or industry focus.

One of the most common pieces of feedback from case reviewers is that a case is too broad in its target discipline as indicated in the IM/TN. New case authors will often note in their IM/TN that their case would be applicable to multiple disciplines which generally is not true for effective cases. The best cases have clear, targeted learning objectives linked to specific theories/ frameworks in a designated discipline. As such, we strongly encourage you to put a lot of thought into what you are trying to achieve through your case, which will organically lead to (most often) a single disciplinary focus. There are examples of multi-disciplinary cases, but those are much harder to craft to balance the multiple perspectives.

THEORY/ANALYTICAL FOCUS

Building on the importance of specificity, it is also important to really think through how your case can be used to teach students. What core instructional element is your case designed to illustrate? If you are crafting a marketing case, will it allow students to think through pricing frameworks or is it more about marketing segmentation? While good cases are written to be thorough in the information provided in the case to allow for robust analysis, it is in the IM/TN where authors need to tie the case narrative into the theory focus. This means that you need to think upfront about what business theory you want to have instructors use when teaching your case and provide them with the grounding in the theory in the IM/TN including an explanation of the theory and supplementary resources for the instructor as well as students. This could include references to textbook chapters, academic articles, and multi-media resources (e.g., YouTube videos).

The advantage of having an unambiguous theory/framework focus is that instructors often are searching for cases for a particular course topic. For example, most strategic management courses will have a class or two on resource-based analysis. Writing a decision case on a company that allows students to explore the application of that particular theory within a designated discipline directly addresses a need for course instructors and will be adopted more readily than a general case that does not provide tailored guidance in the IM/TN deeply linked to that specific theory. Specificity also makes your case more searchable when instructors look through case catalogues for potential cases to include in their course.

STUDENT LEVEL

Another early decision to make is the level of students who you anticipate will be the main users of your case: undergraduates; graduate; or executive students. This decision will be driven primarily by the learning objectives you decide to focus on in your case. The learning objectives are officially articu-lated in the IM/TN, but you need to have them in mind as you develop the case document. For instance, the learning objectives for your case will influence the data you do and do not include in your case. Typically, case authors will know which disciplinary perspective their IM/TN will be from and which specific topics within that discipline will be the focus of the case. Learning objectives that relate to undergraduate level topics will be used primarily by undergraduate students and instructors. More complex topics for graduate students or executives will have more sophisticated learning objectives that build on prior knowledge and, in the case of the executive level in particular, may require interdisciplinary perspectives given the extensive lived experiences of those students. The basic rule is that the more complex the case learning objectives, the higher the target student level of the case.

Although the specific learning objectives for your case may change as you develop it, it is important to be thinking about potential learning objectives early on so you can target your case to the appropriate student level. Remember that cases are almost always used in classroom environments where the whole class is at a certain level; the better you can tailor your case to a specific class level, the easier it will be for instructors to adopt your case. Executive classrooms normally have students who are older with higher levels of real-world work experience, which leads to different case conversations than those of first year undergraduate students. The thoughtful identification of the student level allows you to create a more appropriate teaching plan and case discussion flow in the IM/TN, which will make your case stand out.

POSITION IN COURSE

In partnership with the appropriate student level, great case authors also think upfront about where the case could be positioned in the course. Is it more of an introductory case for students who do not have a lot of experience with case analysis? Is it appropriate for students who are in their last year of their undergraduate degree and already have significant experience with case analysis? Does it contain concepts that are reliant on other concepts having been taught within that discipline (suggesting it be positioned later in the course)? For example, a case on strategy implementation in a capstone strategic management course would likely be positioned after students are taught external analysis, internal analysis, and strategic choice. This point may seem somewhat granular, but great cases are those that think about where they are going to be most effective in a course to augment student learning.

CASE DATA SOURCE OPTIONS

The type of case you decide to write will depend on several factors, including the articulated goals, as well as what opportunities are available to you and what constraints you face. Your goal for writing a case will likely help narrow down which types of cases are and are not an option for you. We will talk about publication requirements in more detail in Chapter 11, but it is good to have a general idea what you want to do with your case prior to getting started writing your case and IM/TN. For instance, many case conferences and publishers strongly prefer decision-based cases, or only accept primary source or field cases.

Field or Primary Sources

A field or primary source case is one where the case author works with an organization to gather original data about the focal issue or question in the case. Typically, the primary data is in the form of interviews with at least one company representative, although ideally several different people provide data. Such cases can be supplemented with public data about the organization, but it is the inclusion of original data for the purpose of the case and the sign-off of the key company representative that distinguishes a field or primary source case. While some of the top case journals have traditionally only accepted primary source cases, that has been shifting over recent years to accept court proceedings as primary data (given participants are sworn in when they testify) or to have special editions for secondary source cases.

Many consider primary cases as the gold standard of case research and the ideal to which authors should aspire. Because field cases let authors work with contacts to determine an appropriate case question or issue, field cases tend to be easier to customize to the selected student level and discipline. Field cases also tend to be more up to date since the data source is current rather than historical. Authors can often get access to data about issues within the organization that are not covered in secondary sources and so cases are richer and the focal question less obvious than in secondary source cases. There is the opportunity to hear from multiple stakeholders (often sought by case journal reviewers) which introduces dynamism into the case and makes it more interesting to read.

Field cases also present authors with important challenges. The first challenge is getting access to the company and developing a key contact to champion your case within the organization. While writing the case is a key focus for you, it is often far lower down the priority list for your company contact who has other work-related tasks that take precedence. Another big challenge is the final step where the company has to sign off that they approve your case for publication; without authorization, case publishers and even case conferences will not allow you to use the case. Cases that are not authorized for use under the company's real name can be disguised with the company's permission, which can sometimes overcome the sign-off barrier (see MacMillan and Woodwark, 2012). In the middle of the process, another challenge of field cases is settling on a focal question or issue upon which the case will focus. Often company insiders want to focus on something other than your chosen focus, or to include too many superfluous ideas, or to make it just a commercial for the company. It takes work to come to a mutual consensus for the case topic and to get buy-in from the company for the author's chosen design for the case.

We will discuss more about how to get started writing a case and how specifically to write a primary source case in Chapters 4 and 5 respectively.

Secondary Sources

Secondary source cases are ones where the author uses no primary data and relies entirely on existing published sources including news media, company websites, business data (e.g., Bloomberg), and any archival data. Obviously, this means that authors are limited to firms and topics that have sufficient information and coverage about which to develop a case. While there are certainly limitations on what you can do with only secondary sources, in our experience many great secondary cases can be done using company and public data together to provide the firm and industry background combined with contemporary news coverage on a specific issue to provide the background on the specific decision or problem at hand. The internet certainly has made this task much easier! For examples of secondary source cases we have published using that strategy, see Schnarr and Rowe (2014) about Tim Hortons or MacMillan and Woodwark (2016) about the Canadian Broadcasting Corporation. However, before you undertake a secondary source case, be sure you understand your target publisher's stance on such cases as many publishers will not accept them or only publish them in special issues. You should also understand what the publisher's expectations are about the type and number of sources you are relying on for your case. Publishers will be more open to secondary source cases that are supported by multiple sources to substantiate your story than if there is only one source or only weak sources. Stick to reputable, documented sources as much as possible to minimize this risk and make sure you keep track of where you are sourcing your data from. Secondary source cases often have far longer reference sections than predominately primary source cases.

Secondary source cases have several major advantages. One of the biggest benefits is that authors do not need a contact or access, nor do they need sign-off from the company to publish the case. This means that even beginner case writers can write cases about famous global companies if they so choose. Quick turnaround means that cases can be completed quickly while topical issues are still front and centre in students' minds. Hence, secondary source cases are typically the first to come out about issues at major companies that have had a lot of media coverage. Cases that show a company in a negative light or address controversial topics are almost exclusively secondary source cases (e.g., Rowe and Schnarr, 2012; Schnarr and Snowdon, 2013).

It is important to recognize that there are challenges associated with secondary source cases. Authors must be able to identify and document the key issue in the case well enough without having any insider information, which is sometimes difficult to do; information related to many key business issues often remains inside the company, even with media coverage. Recall that authors cannot fictionalize any part of the case data, which means authors are limited to the actual data they can document. The other major challenge with secondary source cases is that there are fewer publishing outlets than for primary source cases. Before you begin a secondary source case, make sure you know which outlets will and will not consider your work.

We will discuss more about how to get started and how specifically to write a secondary source case in Chapters 4 and 6 respectively.

Hypothetical Cases

A hypothetical case is one that is not based on real events but on a situation created by the author for a particular reason. Usually, the author has a specific teaching point they want to make but cannot find a real example of it, or the teaching point is more easily made with a fictitious example than a real one. Often hypothetical cases tackle very personal or difficult topics – such as tough ethical choices – where most people do not want to share their story with the author for a real case but that the author feels nevertheless is important for students to discuss. Another reason for using a hypothetical case is to separate the general learning point from any one specific example to show what is and is not generalizable. Remember that a hypothetical case which has no real data source is different from a disguised case (discussed in Chapter 1) which does, but which is not disclosed. A famous (and fantastic) example of a hypothetical case is Joseph Lampel's 1991 *Robin Hood* case, which is used to illustrate general strategy, leadership, and organizational change issues.

The main advantage of hypothetical cases is that authors can illustrate whatever issues they wish without having to find or document a real example. As students are not able to do an internet search to see what the company did, it forces students to really think through and provide analysis on the scenario. The primary disadvantage is that such cases are usually not publishable except in textbooks or in specific disciplines such as accounting.

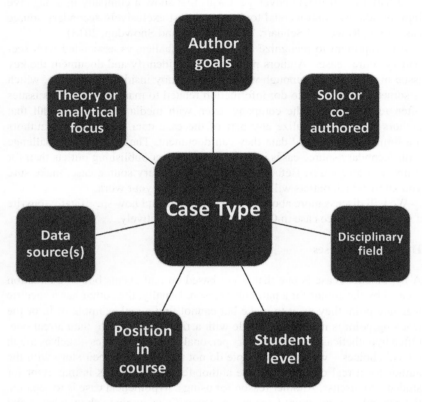

Figure 3.1   What type of case do you want to write?

KEY CHAPTER TAKEAWAYS

- Determining what kind of case you want to write is one of the first steps in case research.
- Upfront decisions that you need to make including whether you are going to write the case by yourself or with co-authors, what your goals are for the case, at what level of student the case should be targeted at and where in the course it should appear, the academic discipline upon which you wish to focus the case, the theory focus, and what type of data source you wish to use.
- We suggest setting goals appropriate to your level and provide examples of relevant goals for the beginner, intermediate, and advanced case writer.

- The more you think through the overarching case writing questions before you start writing the case, the more effective the case will be as a classroom learning tool.

Next, we will discuss how to get started writing your case.

NOTE

1.   Several case conferences have case embryo or cases in development tracks where authors bring early drafts of case introductions and outlines for feedback from other case writers. These tracks are intended to be developmental to help novice case writers learn the craft and develop their case ideas into full cases. See the North American Case Research Association (NACRA) and the Administrative Sciences Association of Canada (ASAC) for embryo case conference opportunities.

4. How to get started writing your case

Now that you have a better idea of the multiple decisions you will need to make to help structure the kind of case you want to write and accomplish your case goals, let us discuss how authors get started writing a specific case. While this can seem intimidating, each case starts with an initial spark that a particular issue, organization, or person (sometimes all three!) would make a great case idea. The rest is up to the case author! Just make sure you do a quick check by going to the website of a case distributor like Harvard Business Publishing or Ivey Publishing to make sure your case idea has not already been done recently before you put too much work into it.

FINDING A CASE ORGANIZATION AND TOPIC

Initially, one of the hardest parts about becoming a case writer is overcoming the belief that it is going to be challenging to find a specific case organization that is willing to collaborate with you and to identify an interesting topic that aligns with your interests and expertise. While it can be challenging, in our experience it is far more accessible than new case writers anticipate. We think understanding the full range of possible ways in which case ideas can come your way helps authors see that there are actually plenty of possible sources. In fact, after you have been writing cases for a while, you may find you have far more case ideas and options than you can possibly complete! Indeed, the challenge most experienced case authors have is how to prioritize their case writing opportunities in the limited time available. We hope we can show you how to spot case writing opportunities all around you so that you always have a new case idea to work on if you wish.

Media Headlines

The easiest way to get started as a case writer is to avoid the challenge of getting access altogether by going the secondary source case route. Keeping up with the news coverage is a fantastic way to spot secondary source case opportunities as you discover key issues facing many diverse organizations. We recommend using public companies for secondary cases since the available data is typically plentiful. You really just need to find reputable coverage of an issue within your area of expertise. For example, a quick look at recent business news in Canada has an article about the CEO of a Canadian bank arguing that given COVID-19 is now more under control, work from home policies are no longer necessary and employees should now be working in the office more often. Should the bank let employees choose where they work (e.g., virtually), or should they require more on-site work? This could be a great case for an organizational behaviour or human resource management class to discuss the merits of on-site and off-site work in relation to productivity, motivation, employee satisfaction, and leadership. Because it is a public company, there will be plenty of background data available. It is also generalizable to a number of different companies, industries, and countries. The point is that if you follow the business news you will start to see many case opportunities about topics in your field that you could explore, which is a terrific way to get started. Just make sure you set an appropriate goal for your case that is consistent with secondary source data. We address in detail how to research your secondary source case in Chapter 6.

Media headlines can also be a way to identify organizations that you may want to contact about a potential primary source case. While some authors might assume that most companies would not be interested in working with them on a case, the fact is you never know until you ask. A case can be an effective way for an organization to communicate its side of a particular story. While they may not agree to talk with you right away, they might agree once the story is no longer in the headlines. We discuss ways to recruit organizations in Chapter 5 on primary source cases.

Friends and Family

Another straightforward way to get started – and the way one of us got started – is to explore case opportunities where the likelihood of your being able to gain access is high. Start with your friends and family members! You probably know plenty of people who run businesses or participate in organizations upon which you can write a case because great cases can be about local small or medium-sized businesses too. Students love to use cases from their region, and you can leverage your contacts to gain access. We have found that friends and family are usually interested in helping new case writers learn their skills. Plus, many such organizations are ones that never imagined anyone would be interested in them, let alone enough to write a case about the firm. It can be a terrific way to get access to an organization for your first primary source case. In return, you can provide the organization with some profile within your school and anywhere else the case is used. The main caveat to working with friends and family contacts is that you have to be sure they really understand that you are not doing free consulting work for them (see below about convincing organizations to participate).

Colleagues and Co-authors

Another great source of potential case contacts is your professional contacts in your disciplinary field including your colleagues and co-authors. These people may know of organizations who might be interested in being the subject of a case and may also know people who can help you try to get access. People in your discipline may also be knowledgeable about firms that are doing interesting things in your field, or who are facing related challenges. Co-authors can be especially helpful in making contacts because they can speak to what it is like to collaborate with you. We recommend telling your professional contacts that you are a case writer (or an aspiring one) who is always interested in hearing about organizations that might be interested in being the subject of a case. You will be surprised that if you keep this up how many possibilities come your way over time.

Students and Alumni

Both current and former students are fantastic sources for case ideas and opportunities as they have often had exposure to case-based learning and recognize the benefits. We make sure all our students know that we write cases and are always happy to hear their ideas. Students, particularly graduate students, can also make great co-authors (see Chapter 10 for information on student-written instructor-facilitated cases). Students can bring interesting organizations to your attention that you might not otherwise know about, and they may have connections that can help you gain access. Graduate students and alumni tend to present especially interesting ideas since they have a deeper understanding of the case method and are better able to spot unusual business practices or anomalies that would make for challenging classroom debates. Alumni are great to talk with too because they tend to have enough experience to be able to identify the practices that are not consistent with what they were taught in school. Such discussions with alumni can reveal to you how your field is changing in practice. Case authors can then incorporate new practices into their cases, which brings the contemporary business world into the classroom. Students who study such cases are then better prepared for what they may face when they graduate to the work world. This is an important way in which case research can help address the much-discussed research–practice gap in management.

We have been approached by many alumni who are interested in writing a case about their current organization, both as an opportunity to use their company in a similar context to what they experienced as students (e.g., in class learning or for student case competitions) and as an opportunity to highlight their company for the current generation of students. Working with alumni on cases is a win–win scenario; it provides an entry into a company for you as a case writer and it allows alumni an opportunity to give back to their institution beyond the traditional means of financial support.

Corporate Sponsors

A key opportunity to identify potential case companies is through your school's fundraising or development office. Companies who sponsor events at your institution like case competitions or who provide funding support for students or academic programmes can be wonderful case contacts because they already have a track record of supporting your school. We make sure our university's corporate development office knows to contact us if any organization expresses an interest in supporting the school more actively than simply donating. We have had tremendous success with this avenue as it is sometimes a sweetener for institutional fundraisers to offer the opportunity to have a case focused on a potential donor organization. We have also worked with our institution's fundraising office to reach out to specific donors who we believe might be interested in working on a case with us. Both pathways have borne fruit for us, but in general the former is the more effective of the two. Similar to working with alumni organizations, we provide examples of cases to potential company partners, so they recognize early on the format and tone of the kinds of cases we write. We are also upfront about the amount of time and types of information we will need from the organization in case that is a deal-breaker for them.

Professional Organizations

Any professional organizations to which you belong are potentially rich opportunities for future case studies. This could include sports teams, charities, recreational facilities, and clubs. If you have a history with the organization, you are already well on your way to a case being written! If they are supportive of a case being written on their organization, these organizations can connect you to other members or their parent organization. They also often have newsletters or other updates where you can spot interesting activities that members are involved in or future plans for the organization (e.g., expansions) that could be a case topic.

Cold Calls

Believe it or not, this can work! We are living proof – see Risavy and Woodwark (2020) and Woodwark and Risavy (2020). These two cases were written for a special issue on women entrepreneurs. We wanted to contribute a case on that subject and cold emailed the leaders of a list of regional firms led by women. We explained upfront why we were interested in talking with their firms and why it was important to have more cases with female protagonists (see Grandy and Ingols, 2016; Sharen and McGowan, 2019). Honestly, we did not expect much, if any, interest. However, we received more responses than we could cover and had to prioritize the firms with whom we wanted to work. In the end, we had two that we really wanted to write about, which resulted in two separate cases. Special calls for cases about underrepresented protagonists and industries are becoming more common with publishers, and we think that the cold call or cold email strategy can work well when you are targeting diverse leaders. They understand the impact of not being represented in traditional curricula. It is important that you are clear from the start about your agenda (and timeline) so people can decide if they are interested under that condition. We have also tried cold calling and emailing for subject cases for case competitions, which again has led to very positive results, particularly when we were able to pair them with a connection to our institution. Recently, we were able to secure a major not-for-profit organization in our region to be the subject of a major case competition, helped by the discovery that the son of the organization's CEO graduated from the business programme at our school (and had an enjoyable experience in one of our classes). Although sometimes we have had to kiss a lot of frogs to find a great case company, we have always been able to find participants using our tricks to convince companies to come on board (see below). Doing some rudimentary homework before making contact is always a good idea.

Cases Come to You

The best-case scenario – and when you know you have really developed a reputation as a case writer – is when case opportunities come to you! People know that you write cases and bring you ideas and contacts that are good leads. This is the ultimate goal for authors who love writing cases. In our experience, it will not take you as long as you think to reach this stage. Keep building your reputation as a case researcher and writer using all the above suggestions.

Final Organization Recruitment Tips

Regardless of how you identify a case opportunity, it is always best practice to provide the organization you are considering working with a few sample cases that you have written or that you often use (and have permission to provide). This allows firms to better understand what you are asking them to participate in and provides some comfort that they will not be maligned in the case. However, we do not also share the instructor's manual/teaching note (IM/TN) since firms do not usually review those and do not need to sign off on them. The bottom line is that recruitment for cases gets easier the more you do it and the more you have sample published cases to share that showcase your case writing abilities.

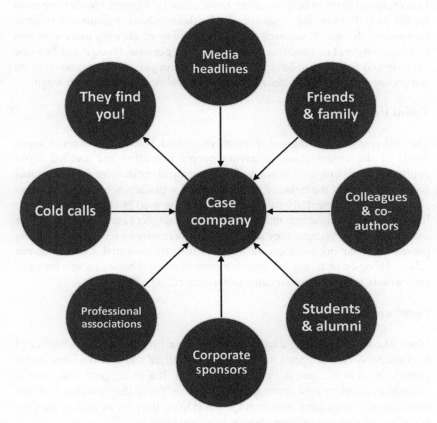

Figure 4.1   How to find a case organization and topic

CONVINCING A CONTACT AND ORGANIZATION TO PARTICIPATE

There are many reasons for companies to agree to be the subject of a case. Some of them might be more apparent than others to your target company. It is your job as an aspiring case writer to help them see the benefits of participation. In return, you will need information, time for interviews and questions, and time to review and approve case drafts from your contact. Outlined below are the key reasons that companies agree to be the focus of cases.

Exposure

One reason to agree to help an author write a case is to garner broader exposure for the firm. Best-selling cases are read by thousands of students and instructors around the world, so cases are a low-cost way of drawing more attention to a company and its products or services. On a personal level, it can be quite exciting and flattering to have a case written about you as a protagonist, so do not underestimate the persuasive power of appealing to your contact's ego!

Talent Recruitment

The first step in the hiring and recruitment process, particularly at more junior levels of the organization, is having people interested and excited about applying to the company. While a case is not an advertisement for a firm, it is one way to get on the radar of students and new graduates in global business schools; this is particularly true if the case will be used in your local area. We have had success attracting major companies as subject cases as part of a large case competition because they saw it as an opportunity to see the top students present on their organization, in order to identify potential students at our school for co-op or future full-time job opportunities. This was a win for us as case writers and a win for students who received job offers.

Legitimacy

Much like a media article, a case can also offer a firm external validation and legitimacy. A case suggests that the firm is credible and that the issue under consideration in the case is interesting and real. It also suggests that there is something novel or new about what the firm is doing that justifies both the attention of management instructors in developing the case as well as the time and effort of students to learn about it in a classroom.

Expression

Some firms and protagonists appreciate the opportunity to tell and share their story. It can be simply so others can learn from their experience. It can also be because there is something unusual or unique about their story. For example, some contacts are motivated to have themselves or their firm represented in a case because their demographic or industry is underrepresented. A case is an opportunity to tell their story from a unique perspective (e.g., entrepreneurship from a female perspective). Authors need to explain to potential case contacts why it is important for students to be exposed to a wide range of decision-maker perspectives and industries.

Focus and Attention on Critical Issue

Collaborating with an author on a case is an opportunity for your contact to focus their attention on the issue at hand. The author will require all the relevant background information about the firm and issue, so the contact has to focus on compiling that data. The author will also ask the contact plenty of questions about the history, context, and current status of the issue. Working with the author on a case can help the protagonist devote time and attention to the issue which may not have happened without external prompting. In fact, the development process of the case can prompt new insights for the case contact before the case is even finished purely as a result of the types of questions being asked by the case writer.

Caveat: A Case is Not Consulting

One important caveat for all primary source case writers: it is important that your contact and the organization understand that a case – or an accompanying IM/TN – does not constitute a consulting engagement. A case author is not – and should not promise to be – a management consultant who provides recommendations to the organization. Live case competitions can pass along students' recommendations to a case company (see Chapter 10), but the case author's job does not include formal recommendations in the way a consulting contract would. Make sure your contacts understand this before committing to be involved.

Additional Resources

If you are still having difficultly convincing a contact to sign on to your case, or if you simply want to provide additional supportive context to your contact, we recommend you share an open letter to case contacts by John Seeger (2012) published in the *Case Research Journal* called 'So they're writing a case – about you! An open letter to the organizational host of a case writer'. This is a brief summary of the many concerns that organizational case sponsors often have about having a case written about their organization and it explains how their concerns can be addressed and why certain case characteristics are important to include in a great case.

HOW TO DETERMINE A CASE TOPIC

If you are writing a primary source case, there are several strategies for how an author and a key contact in the case organization can work together to determine the specific focus of the case.

In some situations, the case topic is evident from the start of the discussions with your contact. Perhaps you reached out to the organization for the purpose of writing a case on a specific topic and they have agreed. Alternatively, the contact came to you with a specific proposal that works, and you agreed. Sometimes the case topic is easy to determine, and you are able to move forward quickly to the next step.

In other situations, the author and contact are mutually interested in writing a case but the particular topic for the case has to be negotiated. It could be that the contact has a clear idea for the case topic and the author has to determine if or how that could work for their own goals. Sometimes it could be a good topic, but the company (for competitive reasons) is not able to provide the specific information that will be required for the case analysis. In other situations, particularly if the case is for a case competition which requires company participation, the team may not be available at that specific time. We once worked with a major international brewing company and had initially agreed to focus the case on the growth in craft beer; however, we discovered early on that the entire craft brewing business unit would be at a corporate retreat during the time of the case competition. This required both the authors and the company to pivot and produce other possible case topics.

There are times when the proposed topic fits with the author's area of expertise and the case the contact wants you to write will work, meaning that the author will also be able to write a complete IM/TN on the topic. However, in other situations the case topic proposed by your company contact is outside your area of expertise. There are a few ways to address this challenge. One option is for the author to pass the case opportunity on to another case writer who has the appropriate expertise to focus the case on the requested topic. Another option is for the author to acquire a co-author who can assist with the IM/TN to provide the needed expertise. Both are good options, and the ultimate choice will really depend on your goals for the case. The final option in this scenario is for the author to try to negotiate with the contact to focus the case on a different topic that is a better fit for the author's area of expertise. In this situation, be sure you do not agree to try to cover both topics in a single case because – rightly or wrongly – IM/TNs must have one sole clear disciplinary focus if you wish to publish your case. Case contacts probably do not understand this condition, so make sure you set yourself up for success with the case you plan to write.

Prior to any commitment to write a case, we recommend the author conduct an interview with the contact asking about many different topics that relate to their area of expertise to see what might be possible. We find that most firms have multiple potential options for cases. Once an author starts asking questions about other topics, the contact almost always has other stories to tell that would work well for a case. For example, if our case contact were to propose a case focus in the operations field, neither of us would do an excellent job writing that case as it is not our area of expertise. However, if we explore other topics with the same firm, we can usually find another topic in strategy or leadership which would also make an effective and engaging case. In that situation, the author has to be persuasive to try to get the contact to agree to an alternative focus for the case that works for both parties. One of our tactics coming into the first case writing meeting with our contact is to ask them to bring to the meeting three or four key issues facing their organization right now that are in our areas of expertise. That channels their thinking ahead of the meeting into areas where we will be likely to have alignment. We will then have an in-depth conversation with the contact about each proposed topic, which allows us to identify which topic is the most important to the company, will align with our academic expertise, and will have relevant data to make the case nuanced and descriptive.

Regardless of how you mutually decide on the topic for your case, the process gets easier with practice. When you come to agreement on the case topic, be sure to confirm it in writing (emails are fine) with your contact. Document your decisions as you go along to keep everyone on the same page. One of the main goals is to eliminate any surprises coming from either side!

If you are writing a case purely using secondary source data, there is a lot more flexibility as you have probably already decided on the case focus as it was part of the original idea for the case. As noted at the start of this chapter, the major piece of advice here is to make sure there has not been a recently published case on your company and topic of choice. In addition, make sure you can find sufficient data on the firm to complete the case before you get too far along on a topic; this is easily done by taking a look at the company's website, doing a good search on the company's name and a scan of recent media headlines, and exploring whether your institution has access to databases and journals that can help you with background research. We recommend using an outline even for secondary source cases so you can see the big picture requirements and progression of the case story you are going to write. Have a colleague peer review it to make sure the flow makes sense. In the event that you want to write about a particular firm but do not initially know the specific topic upon which to focus, we recommend doing secondary research until you find a topic that works for you, and then developing an outline for what the case may look like.

Keep in mind that writing a case of any sort is an iterative process that has to adjust as new information is acquired and as the story you decide to tell develops.

WHAT IS THE STORY YOU WANT TO TELL?

Once you have decided on the topic of your case, the next step is to figure out how to structure the story that you want to tell. Well-crafted cases have a smooth and logical flow to them and an effective way to ensure that happens is through drafting a detailed outline of your case before you begin to write a full draft. Start with a rough outline and get feedback on it early and often from your focal company (for primary source cases) or your co-authors and peers (for solely secondary source cases).

A case outline is a tool that serves three main purposes in the development of your case. First, an outline helps you think through how to structure and express the story of your case. Make effective use of headings to help you think through what information should be provided and the order in which it should be presented. Include lots of notes and questions in your initial drafts until the story begins to take shape when you fill in the gaps. You will find yourself moving sections around as well as adding and subtracting topics as you iterate. It is much easier to do this before the full case has been written!

Second, an outline is a communication tool to ensure everyone involved understands what the case is about and what the finished product is likely to look like. Remember that your primary source case has to be signed off by the company before you can use it, so communication throughout the process is vital to keeping support for the project and your relationship with your contact strong. If you are working with primary case materials in a fairly sophisticated firm, it is important to consider that the firm's legal and communications team may want to review the case content before signing off on your case. So, once your outline is mostly complete and everyone agrees about the direction, it is worth checking whether any other internal unit (e.g., the firm's legal team) needs to review the outline. It is better to address any constraints on the case information based on legal or public relations concerns at the outline stage than at the final written stage. It is heartbreaking to write a full case – or worse, a full case and IM/TN – only to have it shelved by the company's legal or communications team because the topic was deemed to be too risky to disseminate publicly.

Third, an outline is a way to identify and request any missing information that you will need as well as to fact check the information you do have. Include the source of information so your contact knows where you got your facts. You can find a lot of initial information from the company website but recognize that the website material may be outdated and may be skewed in terms of how it is presented. List the missing information that you would like to source from them including materials such as corporate history, organizational charts, company structure, factory and sales locations, products, financial performance, photos, images, quotations from key company representatives, charts, and marketing materials. Tell your contact which information is nice to have and which information is critical to include.

We recommend authors devote a lot of time upfront to developing a thorough case outline in collaboration with your case contact. This helps everyone see the overall decision focus of the case and allows for buy-in from any other firm representatives (e.g., CEO, legal, public relations, etc.). It also ensures consensus and sign-off upfront on the key case focus. We have worked with (thankfully only a few) companies on cases where they suggested changing the case focus after the case had essentially been written. By reminding them about the earlier agreement on the case outline, we were able to pivot them back to the agreed-upon focus. The outline development stage is an iterative one that can take quite a bit of time but devoting that time upfront will save you a lot of time in the writing and approval stages – trust us! The best tool we have found to help you manage the process from case idea to full case storyline is the outline. We simply cannot recommend the outline method enough.

SAMPLE CASE OUTLINE

While each case outline will vary, we have developed a sample general outline below as a starting point for you to use initially. The proposed sections and their order can be changed, depending on what makes the most sense for your particular case. Figure 4.2 provides a sample outline as a guide.

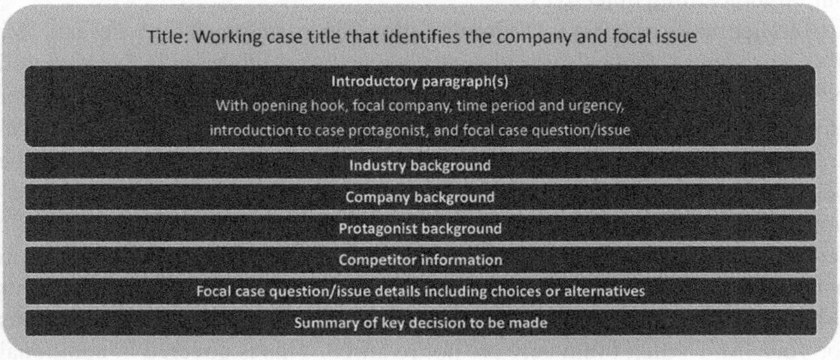

Title: Working case title that identifies the company and focal issue

Introductory paragraph(s)
With opening hook, focal company, time period and urgency, introduction to case protagonist, and focal case question/issue

Industry background

Company background

Protagonist background

Competitor information

Focal case question/issue details including choices or alternatives

Summary of key decision to be made

Figure 4.2   Sample case outline

SETTING YOURSELF UP FOR CASE WRITING SUCCESS

Once you have an accepted outline from your contact (if you are writing a primary source case), you are ready to begin writing the case narrative itself. If you are writing a secondary source case, you can start the case narrative once you are comfortable with the outline, although we recommend getting a trusted colleague to give you feedback on the outline to ensure you have not overlooked anything important. It is tempting at this point to focus solely on the case narrative and some authors are successful with that approach. However, in our experience the next step is to develop the outline for the IM/TN. This is because your case and your IM/TN need to be truly aligned; your case is an extension of learning objectives contained in your IM/TN. Many experienced authors find it is easier to create that alignment by drafting an IM/TN outline before writing the case narrative. This technique also allows you to identify any issues with the IM/TN early enough to adjust the case outline before writing the case narrative. Otherwise, you may find that once you begin the IM/TN you need to change your case plan and rewrite a large part of it. While you work on the IM/TN, keep in mind that you do not have to get the firm to sign off on that part of your work – only on the case itself. We typically do not review our IM/TN outlines or drafts with our case contacts. The instructional side of cases is usually best to review with teaching colleagues rather than with company contacts. Other authors choose to write the case narrative first and then start the IM/TN, so over time you will determine which approach works best for you. We used to write the full case first and then develop the IM/TN, but through experience have switched to writing the IM/TN outline once the case outline is done. Sometimes we even start the IM/TN outline before the case outline is done to help us think through what the case must contain to meet our target learning objectives.

Another tip for success is to closely follow the instructions for cases and IM/TNs from your target publishing outlet. How your submission is received will be dependent on how well you followed the criteria your preferred publisher has outlined for authors. Nothing makes an editor desk reject a case faster than a submission that has ignored the communicated criteria! Give yourself the best chance for a positive reception by paying close attention to all the instructions to authors before you submit your case. Most publishers have a specific set of sections they want (and do not want) authors to cover in their IM/TNs in particular, so make sure you know what the criteria are before you draft your IM/TN outline. This could also save you time and effort by not writing sections for your IM/TN that ultimately are not required. This is covered in additional detail in Chapter 8.

Project and client management skills are also necessary to be a successful case writer. Keep in touch with your contact and communicate next steps and estimated timelines as much as you can. Make sure any outstanding tasks such as information gathering are assigned to someone whom you can contact. Ensure your contact understands your goal for the case. This is important because if your goal is to publish the case in a peer-reviewed journal, your contact also needs to understand how the peer-review process works. Manage expectations so that they know the case may need several rounds of revisions – and possibly even a refocusing of the topic – based on the changes the reviewers wish you to make. Sometimes this involves additional interviews to solicit deeper insights or perspectives. Finally, if you are interested in working with a company for a specific case project (e.g., student case competition or a special topic issue of a case journal), we strongly recommend that you clearly communicate all of the key dates upfront, confirm that your contact (and anyone else required in the organization) will be available and build in some time buffers at the end for approvals.

KEY CHAPTER TAKEAWAYS

- To recap, make sure your case idea has not been done recently before you start developing a new one.
- Authors can choose to write a secondary source case from the media to avoid the challenge of getting organizational access, or they can overcome the access challenge with the help of contacts such as family and friends, co-authors and peers, students and alumni, professional organizations, corporate sponsors, and even old-fashioned cold calling.
- Seasoned case writers often have people bring case ideas to them because they are well known as case authors. Tell everyone you know that you write cases and always appreciate new ideas.
- An author's first job is to persuade a company and contact to participate in their case with them. Companies choose to have cases written about them for many reasons including to gain exposure, to help recruitment, to gain legitimacy, to express themselves, to focus their attention on the chosen issue, and to boost their egos.
- Make sure your contact understands that a case is neither a consulting project that will deliver recommendations nor is it a commercial for the company.
- There are several different ways to decide on the case focus with your contact; once decided, make sure to put it in writing.
- Use an outline for the case to help build buy-in, track missing information, and help you think through the story you want to tell. Upfront investment in developing a detailed outline will save you time and hassle later in the

process. Once your case outline is complete, consider developing the IM/
TN outline before starting the case narrative.

- Be sure to review the case and IM/TN criteria from your target publishing
  outlet before you begin your case narrative and IM/TN.
- Use all your project management and client management skills to keep your
  case on track and to manage expectations with your company and contact.
  If there are deadlines you need to meet (e.g., for a case competition launch
  or a special issue of a case journal), make sure they are communicated
  upfront and you build in buffer timing to make sure you hit your deadlines.
- Finally, remember that the best time to start writing a case is now.

Our next chapter outlines how to research your primary data case.

5. How to research your primary data case

You have decided to write a primary data case where you will be working with an organization and a key contact to research and explain a real situation the organization has faced. In this chapter, we will outline the steps we recommend for making this process as seamless and effective as possible, while highlighting the factors to consider along the way. First, we review what we mean by a primary data case and why you should consider writing one.

WHAT IS A PRIMARY DATA (OR FIELD) CASE?

A primary data or a field case means you are working with a contact to write a case about a real organization to which they belong that focuses on an issue, problem, or opportunity about which the organization actually had to decide in real life. With a primary case, the facts in your case actually occurred and your job is to explain to the reader what the issue is, why it matters, the available alternatives the decision-maker has to address the issue(s), and the overall context for the decision. Recall that the purpose of a primary data decision case is to put your readers in the shoes of the case protagonist, allowing them to experience the process of deciding using an evidence-based rationale. Also remember that the structure and purpose of a primary case and a secondary case are usually very similar; the two case types diverge based on the origin of the source data. Because primary source cases have 'insider' data, they can have more interesting and unique information and address questions that would not be available to outsiders. Thus, primary source cases tend to be more engaging and more exclusive, while also having the added benefits of giving authors the most options in terms of publishing outlets. It is important to point out that writing a field case does not mean that the case relies purely on primary data; it means that the case authors have access to rich, first-person accounts of events, more proprietary company information and a deeper understanding of the background of the issue being described, all of which is supplemented by secondary data that is publicly available.

PRIMARY DATA CASE RESEARCH STEPS

In Chapter 4 we discussed how to recruit organizations for field cases and why they might consider participating. We also mentioned that in addition to writing and research skills, successful primary case writing involves strong project management and consulting skills. Now we will break down the steps in working directly with an organization to create a case in more detail.

Recruiting an Organization and Getting Sign-on

The recruitment process is usually the biggest barrier that new primary case writers face when considering a field case. In our experience, getting access to an organization is actually less challenging than most novice case writers fear it will be. Also, like most things, company recruitment gets a lot easier with practice. Once you have a few published cases under your belt, we recommend showing the finished products (e.g., a copy of a few of your finished, published cases) to the firms you are trying to recruit so they can see what the end product will look like. This method demonstrates to people that you have been successful in the past and are likely to be able to publish another case in the future. It reassures them that you can write well and objectively about other companies. It also provides them with an example of what a finished case looks like as often organizations only have experience with business cases that are plans to get new products/services approved rather than the types of academic decision-based business cases this guide is dedicated to demystifying. You can refer back to Chapter 4 for our recruitment suggestions to help you get your field case started.

The recruitment process is done when you and your case contact – who should have the authority to bind the organization – have agreed in writing that you want to work together on a case about an initial suggested focus (which may change) for the purpose of future publication (or whatever your goal is for the case). Be sure you understand why the organization is participating and what it is they want out of the experience. Knowing your contact's motivations for working on a case with you is important so you can ensure his/her needs are met along the way and minimize the risk that the case will not be completed or signed off. Remember that your goal is eventually to be able to use your case to meet the goal you chose for this project.

Finally, as we have already noted in previous chapters, even though your contact may have the authority to provide final approval for the case, it is worth enquiring early on if that needs to be done in consultation with others in the organization such as the legal or communications departments. Sometimes it is good to have your contact bring them into the loop right at the beginning of the conversation about the case so that they are not surprised after you have spent hours meeting with the organization, doing external research, and writing the case.

Ethics Approvals

In addition to the case approval that you will need to obtain from your partner firm, there could be internal approvals you need to obtain through your home institution, depending on its research policies. One question we often receive from new case authors is whether or not they will need to get ethics or Institutional Review Board (IRB) approval before beginning primary case research. The answer is that it depends on your institution whether or not case research is included in the school's ethics/IRB policy. For some schools, case research activities like interviews are considered the same as any qualitative academic research project and would therefore need approval to conduct the same kind of semi-structured interviews. In that case, the argument is that the activities are the same and therefore the risks and responsibilities are the same even if the final purpose of a case and a qualitative research project are very different. Other institutions take the opposite view and exempt case research (sometimes implicitly and sometimes explicitly) from ethics/IRB review processes. In this view, the school considers case research to be a low-risk, everyday interaction between their faculty or students and the local community, which does not require a research ethics review. Schools who take this approach look at case interviews as one-off activities much like media interviews, which are also exempt in part because the number of people who are interviewed for a case is usually very low, whereas qualitative research projects can have many participants. Of course, other institutions have middle of the road stances on the issue and require a low risk, expedited ethics review for cases but not a full review, a balanced approach which recognizes the difference between the risk level of a major research project and a case project.

Regardless of the rationale of your institution, we highly recommend you understand your school's policy as it applies to case research as much as possible before you proceed, especially given the sometimes lengthy time frames for IRB review processes. As a case author, you can find yourself in the unfortunate position of having to explain to your case contact that the first step in working on the case on which they have just agreed to participate is to wait several months (or longer) for ethics approval from the very institution that approached them! Obviously, this is frustrating for all involved, but all the more reason for you to know what the process is in advance so that you can manage expectations and timing with your contact. Talk to other case writers at your institution about their understanding of the ethics/IRB process for cases at your school, and what the tacit norms are around how strictly they are followed.

Finally, some institutions do not understand case research and may not have a clear stance or have even considered whether they should be part of the ethics process. That is a tough position to be in as you may have to educate the IRB about case research before you gain any clarity. In that case, authors may choose to assume case research is exempt until explicitly told otherwise. This is an area where authors have to decide for themselves their level of risk tolerance. The reality is that the risk level for the vast majority of cases is quite low, although in the era of social media the risk of a negative public relations incident is never zero. Keep in mind that unlike other kinds of academic research papers, we know of no case publishing outlets that require evidence or assurance prior to publication that the case went through the ethics/IRB process at the author's institution. We think this suggests that case publishers recognize the mutual partnership that is required for a field case to come to fruition, and the fact that in the vast majority of cases it is ultimately the organization that holds most of the power in the case author–case subject relationship since any mistreated or unhappy contact can simply end the project and/or refuse to sign off the case for publication. We suspect this practical reality is why most institutions do not (yet?) require ethics/IRB approvals for case research. The other (unfortunate) reason could be that case writing as a research activity is not perceived at the same prestige level as traditional qualitative research to which IRBs are more accustomed. While we would argue that the rigour required to be published in the top case journals is equal to (or even higher than) that of the leading journals in the various business disciplines, it could be the case that IRBs do not consider case research to be proper research and therefore do not require authors to go through the review process.

Working with Case Leads

As we mentioned in Chapter 4, our favourite tool for working with case contacts or leads is the case outline. A case outline provides clarity to everyone about the proposed direction of the case throughout the process. Case writing with case leads is an iterative process of repeated clarification and revision until the case is completed. Outlines are also great tools for making information requests because they show your contact why the information is needed for the story you are trying to tell. Outlines also remind the organization that they agreed to the various sections upfront, which helps prevent case scope creep at the end of the project.

For case leads who work well iteratively on email, case outlines are an effective tool. Some case leads may need you to work with them in other ways because written communication through email is not their preferred communication style. For instance, some busy case contacts are phone people and that's the best way to get their attention when you need it. Scheduling a phone call gets your case on the calendar of your contact to ensure a time to talk through issues related to the case. Many of us are now very familiar with videoconference technologies such as Zoom or Microsoft Teams, which are a nice alternative to the phone because, with the permission of your contact, the calls can be recorded for future reference and do not elicit long-distance charges. Also, documents can be shared on screen during the call, which makes the walk-through of the various case elements much clearer. If you are very fortunate and both you and your contact are in the same geographic area, you may choose to do initial meetings in person to build a stronger connection. Make sure you determine your contact's preferred communication method early on and work with it as much as possible. Of course, at the end of the day you do need your contact to read your case draft in detail and either sign-off on it or indicate the revisions required for sign-off. Our advice is to be flexible with your communications approach when working with case contacts based on what you find effective. You really want to avoid being a hassle for them unnecessarily.

Often, although not always, your case contact is also the case protagonist. If so, one of your goals as a case writer is to get to know your case lead as a person so that you can represent him or her appropriately. Cases are more interesting and effective when readers get a good sense of the protagonist's voice and who they are as individuals. Spend time getting to know your case lead including their academic and work history and any personal elements about them that may have influenced their career choices or influenced their strategic preferences. This type of detail, beyond anything that could be found in an official bio, is what makes primary data cases more dynamic and interesting to readers.

One thing that authors have to do in order to work well with case leads is to explain the purpose of the case (e.g., what are students going to learn through studying the case) and the process authors use to complete it. Case leads will vary in their understanding of the case method, with some having used cases as a learning tool at business school themselves while others having had no exposure. Make sure your contact understands how cases are used in class if they are not sure; if they are local to your institution, invite them to watch a case class being taught. This will help them understand why the focal case decision needs to be so well articulated. Most case leads will not have previous experience with being actively involved in case writing and probably will not be familiar with that process. Make sure your contact understands what your goal is for the case and what that means for the stages and timelines, especially if you are trying to publish it in a peer-reviewed journal where you can expect several rounds of revisions. We find it useful to continually reassure the case lead that no part of the draft case will be used until it gets signed off. It is important to remind them of this when you are discussing whether or not to include any sensitive data in the case. Ultimately, what is and is not included in the case is within the case lead's control. Authors can make requests and recommendations, but in the end the case lead must approve the case document before it can be used. Authors are therefore very motivated to ensure the case contents are to the lead's liking. That said, cases are not intended to be advertisements for firms; authors are responsible for providing a balanced perspective on the firm in the case narrative.

Interviewing Strategies

Interviews are the *sine qua non* of primary case research and part of what makes these cases so much fun to write. In most circumstances, the bulk of your interviews will be with your primary contact or case lead. In our experience, it usually takes two or three one-hour interviews with the case lead (and other relevant company contacts and stakeholders) to get the required information to write the case, along with secondary sources such as company publications, websites, financial analyst's reports, and media coverage.

We have developed some best practices for our interview procedure that have served us well over the years. It starts by setting the expectation with your case lead that you will need to schedule several interviews spaced apart so you can follow up after doing more research and writing. For your initial interview, we recommend bringing along your business card details, information about the case development process, a sample case you have written, a sample case release form, and maybe a school brochure or a course outline if the case is for a particular class. We strongly recommend that you have done most of your secondary research prior to meeting with your case lead for the first few interviews. You want to ensure that you are using everyone's time well and respectfully, so make sure you are well prepared and stick to the amount of time you initially booked. It is much better to follow up with your contact later with an additional interview than to try to fit everything into one long session. This also has the advantage of being able to ask more specific questions in the second or third interview than during one long session where you have not had time to absorb what you have already been told.

In terms of the logistics of the interview itself, be sure to request permission to record the interviews, either by audio or video. Audio recordings work well using any tool that automatically creates a searchable transcript (e.g., Zoom or Otter). Searchable transcripts are very useful to case writers because when you are writing your case, you can search by topic and easily find the information you are looking for. Make sure your interviewee knows that the interviews and transcripts will not be shared with anyone besides your case writing team; interview data and transcripts should also be properly stored in a secure environment and disposed of at the appropriate time post case-writing in a secure manner. In the event that you cannot get permission to record the interviews, take as detailed notes as you can. This is where it is helpful to have a co-author as you can both take notes to ensure the fulsome capture of data. Consider, though, that this might be an indication that your contact is not fully committed to the case process, or that he or she may need to address an issue with you before you continue. In our experience, case contacts who are committed to the case are comfortable with our recording any interview, so if your contact hesitates, think about what you can do to resolve any discomfort before proceeding.

Good interviewing is a balance between the questions you have prepared in advance and those that emerge from listening to the story your contact is telling you. The type of interviews that work best for case research are called semi-structured interviews where researchers set an advance agenda and set of questions for the interview but are free to respond openly with impromptu follow-up and clarification questions. Case researchers can showcase all their qualitative research skills during the interview process; there are plenty of resources about how to conduct one-on-one interviews effectively depending on your discipline (e.g., Galletta, 2013). In our experience, the one-on-one format works best for cases since case writers are typically focusing on the viewpoint and understanding of one single protagonist. However, there could be situations where you might want to interview a pair of contacts at once, for example firm co-founders. Usually, one or two people constitute the bulk of interviewees for one case, although occasionally you may need to follow up with other individuals for specific points. For example, we wrote a case on an international consumer packaged goods manufacturer for an undergraduate student case competition. While the case had a product development and growth focus, it was helpful to talk to employees involved in product development, supply chain, sales, finance, and marketing to understand any potential organizational constraints for any proposed solutions. Speaking with multiple sources has the added benefit of providing the author with a sense of data reliability.

While it is critical that you understand your case lead and protagonist's perspective before you write your case, it is also important to be able to understand the situation from other perspectives as well, as case focal decisions usually involve understanding multiple perspectives. Ideally, your case contact will either be able to articulate the alternative perspectives related to the focal decision or will be able to put you in touch with someone who can help you understand it. Sometimes that will be another member of a management team, or an employee or colleague who might also be willing to talk with you. Other times, this competing perspective will come from the same case lead describing the internal debate he or she experienced. Make sure you represent everyone's perspectives as clearly and as fairly as you can with a view to expressing them in their own voice where possible. In Chapter 2 we outlined the importance of interesting cases having tension; multiple perspectives help develop that tension. Cases where everyone agrees about everything, especially the proposed course of action, are not very interesting to students and are hard to sustain discussion over a full class. A best practice is to make sure all interviewees agree to be fully identified in your case as the source of information, and to ensure that interviewees have the opportunity to review and approve any direct quotations that you use in the case.

A final best practice is to ensure that your interview captures not only factual information about the case question, but also some personal colour about who your interviewees are as individuals. Your protagonist and any other supporting voices in your case are people first, with work experiences and non-work lives that make them interesting to read about. Be sure to learn about who your interviewees are beyond simply their work roles, such as any hobbies, volunteer work, unique experiences, or activities – anything that will bring them to life as rounded individuals. Sharing information about yourself and your personal story is helpful in getting your interviewees to open up and enrich your ability to represent them fully in your writing.

Managing Timelines

A key part of your job in managing expectations with your case lead is communicating important timelines and constraints. We strongly recommend making your timing goals very clear from the start of the process so contacts can understand what you are working towards and can advise you whether or not your timelines also work for them. You can use the case outline to help you manage timelines, or you can establish a separate project plan with deadlines. Your timeline is going to be a direct result of how you intend to use your case; setting expectations about timelines is especially important for case writers who are facing strict journal or publishing deadlines such as a case call for a special topic issue. The best strategy here is transparency and repeated clarification about the goals for your case and the timeliness you need to meet.

It is good practice at the first meeting with your case contact to lay out the expected timeline for the project and its main stages. For instance, upon initial sign-on, explain to your contact your preferred process and the length of time you expect each step to take. This may vary situation by situation depending on how much time you are able to devote to the case along the way. If you are writing a case in the summer when you might not be teaching, your timelines for turning around an outline and first draft are likely to be shorter than if you are writing a case during the busy fall or winter semesters. Remember that your case contact may have times like year-end or around product launches where they are busy and unavailable for interviews or to review case drafts. Keep in contact with your case lead and update him or her on your progress so he or she knows when you will need their time next. This is especially important if you are unable to meet a previously communicated commitment for a deliverable. Sometimes this is unavoidable, and our advice is to let your contact know right away that there will be a delay and provide a new estimated delivery time as soon as possible. Likewise, ask your case contact to communicate in the same way with you, although you will probably have to take the lead in managing that process. The bottom line is that on-going communication between a case writer and the case lead is critical for the success of your working relationship and your project.

Disguising Data

When working with primary cases, the question of whether to disguise some or all of the data in the case may be raised. Most often, when data is disguised in a case, it is limited to specific information; for instance, only the firm financials or names of individuals portrayed in the case are changed. Ideally, case writers negotiate agreements about any disguised data upfront so they can be managed throughout the writing process. As a case author, the important element is to provide the information necessary for students to do the analysis required in the case. There are multiple ways to disguise data in a case. When we have received pushback from companies about data, we sometimes remind them when the data are already in the public domain (e.g., annual reports), which takes away some of the anxiety.

However, even when you have been transparent about the use of specific data in the case and have received preliminary approvals, requests for disguises can come up during the later stages of the case writing process before the case is signed off. This is often due to contacts or their legal or public relations teams getting cold feet about certain disclosures. In that scenario, authors need to consider carefully what are nice-to-have versus need-to-have data disclosures for them to meet their goals for the case. For instance, private companies are often reticent about disclosing real sales volumes or financial data for competitive reasons. In the latter situation, authors need to determine if not having financial data is a deal breaker for meeting their case goals, or whether their goals can be met using disguised financials instead. Continuing this example, instead of providing the actual raw numbers, they could be inflated (or deflated) using a consistent multiplier across all categories or they could be percentages of the total. You could use margins to explain the financial relationships along the supply chain.

Other times, case sources may be reluctant to reveal their real names in a case, or even to reveal the true company name. Again, authors facing this situation must decide whether their goals can be met using a disguise, or whether disclosure is imperative for the case to proceed. We recommend that before you make a deal about disguising information in your case, you check with your preferred publishing outlet to understand the consequences of any disguises to your potential publication. For instance, a journal editor can let you know if disguising a firm name or other details is acceptable from their perspective. It is rare to see published cases where all of the data in the case has been disguised, although this can happen when a case is originally approved and published, and then at a later date (post-publication), the company withdraws its approval. Sometimes this occurs if the leadership at an organization changes. Case authors can work with the case publisher to disguise the case completely so that it is no longer identifiable in any way as the original firm. The advantage of this approach is that case learnings are kept intact, although a lot of value can be lost as a very disguised case can begin to feel like a hypothetical or fictional one.

Unfortunately, requests for disguises tend to come towards the end of the case process when authors are seeking case sign-off and firms or contacts become reticent about revealing their full stories. While it is hard to prevent this situation completely, it is good practice always to confirm with your contact throughout the process whether the information as drafted in the case is something they are in fact comfortable seeing in print. This repeated confirmation process can help prevent last-minute censoring of important details from your case. Although tricky and stressful for authors, remember that dealing with requests for disguised data is preferable to not receiving sign-off to publish your case, so it is wise to do what you can to address such final concerns before you get to the finish line of a published case. We recommend viewing disguises as a compromise that allows your case to move forward, albeit in a different format than originally intended. Whenever possible, we recommend that novice authors do not volunteer or agree to case disguises unless absolutely necessary, because disguises can complicate not only the case but also the IM/TN and the teaching plan.

Personal Experience

Case authors sometimes wish to write cases based on their own personal experiences. This type of case is most commonly submitted to conferences and developmental streams or crafted to be used as in-class exercises such as midterms or final exams. Such cases have their place, but in our experience are rarely published in major outlets because they encompass a single voice and reflect a single perspective. That being said, they can incorporate important teaching and learning moments. Sometimes authors view personal experience cases as a type of secondary source data since they do not have to interview others in order to write them. However, in our opinion, personal experience cases are not secondary source cases since there are usually no published sources used to document the data. For that reason, we see personal experience cases as a special form of primary data cases where the case protagonist and case author are one and the same individual (similar to auto-ethnographic academic research). Often, personal experience cases also use disguised information (e.g., creating a fictional identity for the protagonist), particularly if the case context is controversial or sensitive. If you are considering writing a personal experience case, we recommend contacting the editor of your target outlet in advance to ensure they accept such cases and how they want you to treat the data source.

Case Sign-off or Release Form

The final step in any primary source case is receiving the official sign-off from someone who has the authority to bind the company. Ideally, the sign-off comes from your main case contact with whom you have been working all along and with whom you have built a strong relationship. As previously noted, sometimes your case contact will need to obtain permission from someone else in the organization, such as legal counsel, prior to signing off themselves. For most journals or conferences, the sign-off form is straightforward, although not universally accepted so make sure you obtain the applicable form for your outlet. At the end of this chapter is a sample case release form from the Administrative Sciences Association of Canada (ASAC) that covers the basic requirements. Always check with your publisher or conference for a specific form they require, as most have their own version, and be sure to keep a copy of the signed form in electronic format should you ever need to provide it again. Another example from Ivey Publishing can be accessed at www.iveypublishing.ca/s/publish/ready-to-publish. Most outlets provide the required sign-off form on their websites under author resources.

Additional Information

One of the challenges that primary case writers have is presenting a balanced view of the organization (i.e., not overly positive like a company advertisement) while still keeping the company and contact happy enough with how you represent them so that they will agree to release the case for use. Case leads sometimes appreciate the need for a balanced perspective and will provide objective information about organizational challenges to help you with this issue. Other contacts or sometimes public relations or legal teams

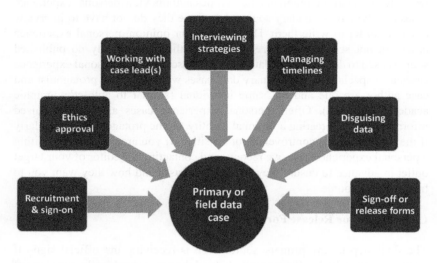

Figure 5.1   Research steps for a primary or field data case

will resist the inclusion of any data that makes the organization look less than stellar, even if it has already been documented in the public domain and is part of the organization's history.

If you face the latter situation, there are a few strategies you can use to try to balance out your case. First, you can explain the need to show the company and issue in a realistic manner, so students trust that the case data is honest and authentic rather than overly manufactured. Sometimes explaining that students will quickly find any negative information about the company through secondary sources and that case users value transparency can help convince your contact to let you include less than flattering data. Students regularly google the subject company of their case (even though we ask them not to) and any negative media (current or historic) is often at the top of the search engine, or on a Wikipedia page. An experienced case writer can refer to past organizational or financial challenges in a balanced way using neutral, non-judgemental language. The issue does not need to take up a lot of space in the case, but it does need to be referenced so that students do not feel the case is a romanticized view of the organization. We have accomplished this balance by using publicly available news releases from the company or letters to shareholders in annual reports that already contain approved quotations about past issues from a senior leader at the organization. Second, if the company is still reluctant, it can sometimes be more palatable if the negative data comes from third-party media sources rather than from the company. In other words, try substituting a secondary source to make an important point rather than a primary source.

A final strategy is to exclude the offending information from the case itself but to include it in the IM/TN for case instructors to raise in the class discussions. While not ideal, since normally authors should include all data relevant to the suggested analysis in the case itself, authors may not have much of a choice if they want the case approved for publication. Since companies do not have to sign off the IM/TN, authors can include secondary source data there as part of the background research or teaching plan. Most publishers have restricted access to IM/TNs so it is unlikely that your case company or lead will access a copy of your IM/TN. The bottom line is that cases work best when they provide a fair and balanced view of a firm rather than an overly positive one. A key challenge authors face is building in that balance in a way that is acceptable for the contact and ultimately results in the official sign-off on the case so it can be submitted for publication.

KEY CHAPTER TAKEAWAYS

- Great field cases are the foundation of the case method, one of the most common pedagogical methods in contemporary business schools. The future of this method of learning truly depends on the quality of new primary cases that authors produce.
- Overall, a successful primary data case is grounded in the author's relationship with the case lead.
- Writing a primary data case requires authors to use their project management and consulting skills throughout the process in addition to their research, writing, and analytical skills. This is why field cases are a challenging and time-consuming endeavour.
- Despite the many challenges of writing primary cases, publishing new field cases is one of the most important ways authors can contribute to furthering their discipline so that there continue to be new relevant cases that accurately portray the issues students will later face in the organizations they will join after graduation.
- Primary cases are management education's greatest source of insight into real organizational decision-making since the vast majority of firm decisions will never be sufficiently documented solely through secondary sources.

Our next chapter addresses how we can write cases about important organizational decisions when we can only do so through secondary sources.

APPENDIX: SAMPLE CASE RELEASE FORM[1]

Case release form
Administrative Sciences Association of Canada (ASAC)

Date:_____

I have read the case entitled:_____
and I hereby authorize the use of the material in this case supplied by my organization. I agree that the case can be used as is. If I have indicated below that changes are required, I release the case once those changes are implemented. I have the requisite authority to take this action.

I understand that this case may be tested in a classroom and may subsequently be modified in the future, though not in a material way. Also, the case may be changed to correct grammatical and typographical errors or to improve flow. I do □ or do not □ wish to review any such changes.

This case is released: without change □
                         with corrections[2] □

Signature:_____

Position:_____

Company:_____

NOTES

1.   Reproduced with permission.
2.   Corrections should be given under separate cover.

6. How to research your secondary data case

In the last chapter we presented why it is a great idea to write primary data or field cases. However, sometimes it is just not possible to get a contact or consent from a company you really want to write about, or to get approval to write about a particular topic. For most large public companies, such as the Fortune 500, it is very difficult to get consent for a primary data case unless you happen to have an existing relationship with a senior executive or you are a famous professor from an elite institution. As we discussed in Chapter 2, cases about well-known companies are interesting and popular, so there is an important place in the case literature for secondary source cases. For case writers, primary and secondary source cases pose a different set of challenges and rewards. We certainly encourage authors to try both types provided they are clear about their goals. Both types of cases can be great fun to write and can help you make an important contribution to your discipline.

WHAT IS A SECONDARY DATA CASE?

A secondary source case is one that relies exclusively on existing data sources such as media articles, databases, books, and websites. To be very clear, primary data cases use information from both first-person interviews and public sources, while secondary source cases rely exclusively on public sources. Secondary source cases avoid the issue of obtaining access and participation from the company itself and also circumvent the need for sign-off. In our experience, secondary cases can be written within a shorter time frame because authors are not reliant on anyone else to complete the work. Needless to say, these are huge advantages compared to field cases. Add to this list the fact that many of the best-selling cases are secondary cases about famous firms and such cases are even more appealing. Many new case writers choose to begin by writing secondary source cases in order to help them get a case published fairly quickly. This can be an effective strategy, but keep in mind that in general there are fewer (but an increasing number of) outlets willing to publish secondary cases. Do your homework beforehand to ensure your target outlet accepts such cases and that your case topic has not been previously published.

SECONDARY DATA CASES

The biggest challenge with secondary source cases is that you have to find a focal decision at your chosen company that is well documented enough to provide a fulsome picture of the case scenario, and whose implications match your or your co-authors' areas of expertise well enough for you to be able to complete an entire instructor's manual or teaching note (IM/TN). As discussed in Chapter 4, sometimes ideas for secondary source cases are easy to spot from media articles about topics that clearly relate to your discipline. News media headlines are an excellent place to start for relevant case ideas. As we have mentioned before, we strongly recommend that case authors in search of new ideas regularly scan the headlines for stories that relate to their disciplinary fields. As secondary source cases require multiple data sources to document the facts, authors will need to look for topics that are covered in multiple outlets. It is unlikely that you will be able to publish a case based on very few sources about the topic. Ideally, you want a topic that has enough coverage that you are not overly reliant on one data source, and for which you will be able to access verified information about the company and potentially the industry. Typically, this means that it is easier to write secondary cases about public companies than about privately held companies (which includes most small and medium-sized enterprises), but that can vary. Other types of firms that have high disclosure practices such as large not-for-profit organizations (NPOs) can also have sufficient data available to outsiders for case authors to be able to craft a strong demonstrable narrative. We provide information in this chapter about how to find information about these types of organizations.

We recommend authors do a preliminary 'proof of concept' research exercise on their case idea before delving too deeply into the actual writing. This includes a quick google search on the organization to see what pops up and, as noted earlier, doing a check for recently published cases on your proposed topic and organization. As we have suggested in other chapters, you may even want to reach out to the targeted publication outlet to see if there is a case close to approval, particularly if it is a hot topic at a popular organization. We actually took this step a number of years ago when we had started gathering information to write a case on the emergence and growth of Beyond Meat, Inc. It was a good thing we reached out to our potential publishing target about this project before we had put a lot of time into it as they let us know that they had already received a case on the company that was about to be published!

Once you have determined that your topic and company are good to go, a case outline can be helpful for authors to ensure that the data they will need to substantiate all the required elements in the case are in fact available before the case writing starts. It is not uncommon for authors to have to pivot somewhat the focus of their case based on the data found in the initial research. It is much better to know upfront the limitations to the available data and adjust the topic or focal case question accordingly. In fact, sometimes authors can stumble on even better ideas through the initial data process, so do not be too quick to settle on your first topic idea.

WHERE TO OBTAIN DATA

Other than original primary data, all other sources of existing data are fair game to include in a secondary source case so long as they can be properly cited and accessed by others. We outline the main data sources below, but each case will have unique potential sources (e.g., patent applications, annual reports, etc.). The most common sources of data we look to when writing secondary cases are from the company itself, news media, social media, scholarly articles, databases, books, professional associations, podcasts, and market research data. We address referencing in more detail below but note that when creating a secondary source case, being able to demonstrate and reference the sources of all the information in your case properly is of the utmost importance. An important practice for successful publication of these cases is meticulous record-keeping of where you sourced all the information you are including in your case. We recommend you develop a system for keeping track of your data collection right from your preliminary exploration as it can be difficult and time-consuming – if not downright impossible – to document your sources properly after you have done a lot of the work. This challenge is particularly true if you have stepped away from writing the case and IM/TN for any period of time. Organization is a vital skill in all secondary source cases!

The following sections provide additional detail about the main data sources you will use when crafting your secondary data case and IM/TN. While we present the information below in terms of how it relates to your focal company or topic, all of these sources could also be used if you need to gather information on competitor companies, products, or services. Moreover, they could all be used to supplement your primary data cases as well!

Company Websites

The website of your focal organization should be the very first place you go to source information for your case and IM/TN. It will be one of the best sources of information for your case and we recommend you scour its contents thoroughly as one of your first research tasks. Bear in mind that information on websites is not always up to date, nor is it a balanced representation of the company. Nonetheless, the firm's website is one of its primary communication tools and will contain invaluable initial information for your case. Here, you can access information including the company's history, vision and mission of the organization, current and past annual reports, earnings presentations, media releases from the company, reports to investors, organizational charts, number of employees, geographic locations, company products, and other related information. If you are writing about a publicly traded company, there is often a section specifically for shareholders from which you can get a sense of the key messages they are trying to convey about organizational performance, the company's current and future strategic direction, and recognized internal and external risks. The letters to shareholders from the Board Chairperson and the CEO in annual reports are a great place to pull quotations to include in your case; this is also true of media releases published by the company. We will address other third-party sites that will have information about your company, but the company's website is indubitably the place to begin!

If your company is publicly traded, another great source of information is documents that the company has filed with regulatory agencies such as the United States Securities and Exchange Commission (SEC). These will often appear on the company's website, but you can also look through the SEC's online Electronic Data Gather, Analysis & Retrieval (EDGAR) online database, which is a searchable database of filed documents for public companies available at www.sec.gov/edgar.shtml. It is publicly accessible for free and contains detailed information on publicly traded companies which often goes back many years. Companies in the EDGAR database are searchable by company or fund name, ticker symbol, central index key (CIK), state, country, or standard industrial classification (SIC). Other countries have similar databases; for example, in Canada the equivalent database is the System for Electronic Document Analysis and Retrieval (SEDAR), which is available at www.sedar.com/homepage_en.htm.

In the United States, even though most NPOs are not required to pay taxes, they are required to complete and file an annual tax return with the Internal Revenue Service (IRS), which is normally done through completing a Form 990. This form includes financial information for the current and prior year, the mission of the organization, and identifies key members of the board and organization (including their remuneration). If you are thinking about writing a case on an NPO, a good place to begin is the IRS' robust searchable tax-exempt organization database available at https://apps.irs.gov/app/eos/. This free database allows you to search by organization, city, or state and in some cases includes international organizations. You can also get started by googling 'Form 990' followed by the organization's name followed by the year you are interested in exploring. For other countries, we have also tried searching the name of the NPO followed by 'tax information'. While it can be hit or miss, it is worth a try!

Further on in this chapter we will discuss other databases and market research sources that can augment information provided on the company's website. Before we leave the topic of company information, we also wanted to mention that one potential source of data is the professional and industry associations to which your company belongs. In fact, sometimes the professional or industry association itself could be the subject of your case (see Woodwark et al., 2020a). The websites of professional and industry associations often contain great overview data related to the subject area about which you are writing. For example, we wrote a case on a convenience store in Ontario, Canada (Woodwark et al., 2020b) and used a lot of information from the Canadian Convenience Stores Association for industry data.

Traditional News Media: Print and Broadcast

There is no doubt that conventional news media has been radically transforming over the last 20 years. In most developed countries, we have shifted from printed daily newspapers and network news broadcasts at fixed times of day to primarily online media channels. Even with this shift, traditional print news media such as newspapers and magazines are one of the best sources of case ideas and data for secondary source cases. Sometimes data from these sources are key to your case because the articles you are using directly refer to your focal issue at the case firm. Other times, authors can use these sources to support their case by providing current background information about the firm, how the focal issue has been examined in other firms, or about the protagonist's background. Remember that converging data from multiple reputable sources makes for a more convincing argument than a single article or a questionable source, so do include a range of sources whenever possible. Make sure you reference only reputable sources and keep track of the dates you accessed articles if using online versions rather than hard copy. Be mindful of the fact that online articles can change or even disappear, so keeping copies of key pieces you need for your case is wise.

Your institution may provide access to direct newspaper archives and media databases such as Nexis Uni and Factiva which are searchable databases of international news information. ProQuest One Business is a searchable tool for business and management publications. In addition, some case topics, firms, or protagonists may have relevant recordings available from television or radio interviews; often they are posted on the webpage for the news site (although sometimes behind a paywall). If your chosen topic is high-profile enough, consider searching for applicable video or transcript data. Online video sources such as YouTube may also have video highlights from broadcast media as well as original sources. However, remember to always consider the credibility of your sources when choosing data to include in your case.

Social Media

Data from social media sources such as Twitter, Facebook, Instagram, and even TikTok are increasingly potential sources of case data as well as ideas, particularly if they have direct ties to your subject organization or protagonist. Depending on your discipline, data from these sources may or may not be the main focus of your case. Certain fields like marketing, public relations, or corporate communications lend themselves to cases based on social media data. Other fields might use social media data as background on the case firm or protagonist (e.g., currently Elon Musk at Tesla, SpaceX and Twitter). A big advantage of social media sources is that they can help case authors clearly demonstrate controversy related to their case and to document the various points of view expressed. Once again, be very careful to consider the reliability of the source you are using so that you are not unintentionally relying on misinformation or disinformation. These sources also need to be properly referenced. Data on these types of platforms are at higher risk of being changed or disappearing, so track and record access dates and keep copies or screenshots of necessary material for your case.

If you are planning a case that relies very heavily on social media data, you might consider contacting the editor of your target outlet for advice on the publication's perspective or policy on basing cases primarily on social media sources. As organizations shift communication channels away from news releases towards more tweets and Instagram stories as a way of engaging with the media, customers, and the broader public, it is certainly becoming more possible and likely that cases will focus on social media data; however, we have not yet written or reviewed such a case and are uncertain how they will be received by editors. Consider reaching out for input at your chosen outlet in advance so you know sooner rather than later if such sources are sufficient for publication of a secondary source case. Another way to address publishing outlet concerns about relying on social media data for a case is to incorporate coverage from traditional media as well. For example, sometimes important social media events get covered by traditional media too, so case authors can supplement their sources by using both types. It will be interesting to see how social media sources are or are not normalized in twenty-first-century case writing. In general, case outlets are becoming more open to new case formats (see Chapter 10 on special cases). As social media continues to be a forum where controversy is expressed and to which organizations have to respond and react, we see a lot of potential interesting cases stemming from such data.

Podcasts

A new and interesting source of potential case data is podcasts. There are a number of podcasts related to firms that could be used as the basis for a written case or as supporting data for background. Since the growing popularity of podcasts is fairly recent, it is currently unclear whether publishing outlets are open to authors who seek to write cases based on a podcast episode. The second author based a case submitted to a recent North American Case Research Association (NACRA) conference on a podcast source and it generated some debate about the eligibility and value of such a strategy. For instance, one reviewer pointed out that converting a podcast question to a case format would be likely to add little additional value from the students' perspective and that wise instructors would simply assign the podcast itself instead (see Chapter 10 about podcases). Given that students may well prefer to listen to a podcast than read a case based on it, the reviewer may well be right. We think that outlets like publishers and case conferences will need to establish policies or recommendations about best practices when using podcasts as case sources. In the meantime, we recommend consulting with the editor of your target outlet prior to investing much work in a 'podcast-based case' to ensure the outlet will in fact consider such a case. Thinking a bit more broadly, a case author, where permitted by copyright, could still refer to a podcast in the IM/TN as a case pre-listen, if it supplements the case, rather than supplants it.

Books and Scholarly Articles

Books about your company, industry, or protagonist could also be helpful for case writing. For example, biographies can be great data sources for cases about the leadership of various well-known individuals. Books on particular firms or industries can be terrific sources of historical background that may not be available elsewhere. In the information age, authors can easily overlook the fact that the good old-fashioned book is still a wonderful resource for case writers!

Scholarly articles from published journals can also support your case. Typically, journal articles will not be key sources of your case data, but they can help authors provide background data about an issue, an industry, or particular firms. Scholarly articles can be helpful in writing the case content itself if you happen to find ones relevant to your topic. Just remember that the formatting guidelines for writing a case are different from those for writing a traditional journal article in that you don't use normal citation protocols (e.g., Woodwark and Schnarr, 2022) in the body of the case but rather provide the appropriate reference in either footnotes or endnotes.

However, scholarly articles are vital to the accompanying IM/TN for your case in almost all scenarios. This is because one of the functions of an IM/TN is to link the specific topics in the case to the broader related literature. Many outlets have required sections for scholarly references in their IM/TN templates. Some outlets will only require you to cite the sources of information you are using in your IM/TN, while others require authors to list and annotate key scholarly articles related to your case for instructor background or student reading assignments. We will address the IM/TN in detail in Chapter 8 including additional information about how to incorporate scholarly articles, but it is worth pointing out that they can be important sources for your cases in multiple ways.

Databases and Market Research

Databases can be important sources of information for your case depending on your disciplinary field. For fields where industry background is important, proprietary databases such as Bloomberg, MarketLine, or Nielsen can provide historical and comparative financial data or market share. Check with your institution's librarian to find out the databases to which you have access. Other databases like national statistics are (at least in part) publicly available (e.g., Statistics Canada, United States Census Bureau, National Institute for Statistics, Geography and Informatics in Mexico).

In addition, market research data can provide helpful background information about your firm and its industry. While some market research data is publicly available, much is proprietary either as stand-alone products or incorporated into broader databases. As examples, Passport is Euromonitor's market research data for countries and companies, while IBISWorld provides industry market research reports. For country-level, socio-economic, and geo-political information, the World Factbook (which is regularly updated) is a free online source for over 250 world entities available at www.cia.gov/the-world-factbook/. Similarly, the Political Risk Yearbook (developed by Political Risk Services) provides comprehensive reports for more than 100 countries with helpful information, particularly about cases related to market entry or international expansion; again, this source is proprietary, so check to see if your institution has a subscription. These sources can be particularly helpful in finding information for background sections of your case. Check with the librarian at your institution(s) to find out what databases and market research sources you or your co-authors may have access to.

Government Proceedings and Records

One of the benefits of writing a case now as opposed to decades ago is that many government proceedings and records are freely available online. If you are writing a case on a recent situation where the company appeared or testified before a government committee, it is worth spending a little time to see whether the transcript is available online. In fact, many case publishing organizations look favourably on secondary data cases that use sources from presentations to government bodies, particularly if the participants have to be sworn in to testify. As an example, the UK Parliament's Parliamentary Archives has a very comprehensive database (parts go back to the year 1715!) of parliamentary debates in the House of Commons and the House of Lords, including written transcripts, available at https://archives.parliament.uk/online -resources/parliamentary-papers/. While some of this is available free of charge, part of it is only available through their subscription service, UK Parliamentary Papers (check to see if your library has a subscription). Similar access is available in the United States and Canada for their government proceedings and are sometimes also available at the state and province level.

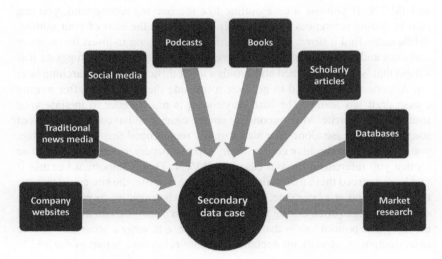

Figure 6.1   Where to obtain secondary data

REFERENCING

With all these sources of data available to you as a secondary data case writer, one of the biggest challenges you will face is keeping track of it all so that you can cite your sources properly throughout. It is hugely important that you accurately attribute the source of information you are using in your case and IM/TN and that you cite it in the manner requested by your publisher. Remember that references from secondary published sources are important because they show to the reader – as well as reviewers and editors – that the case data is in fact real rather than hypothetical. Having thorough sourcing for secondary data cases also demonstrates to the potential case publisher that you have used accurate and legitimate information in the crafting of the case and IM/TN, which minimizes third-party risk at their end related to the information in the case. The fact that the information has already been documented elsewhere is why publishing outlets do not require sign-offs for secondary source cases.

The number one tip we can give you is to find out from the start of your project the referencing format required by your target outlet – both whether they want endnotes or footnotes, and any specific referencing style they require (e.g., Harvard, APA, MLA, Chicago, etc.). Even if it is not a format you are familiar with, there are online tools to convert citation formats easily, so find one you like or ensure you have a good style guide. The best thing you can do to make your case ready for submission to your chosen outlet is to start using the format they want you to use as soon as you begin to write your case and IM/TN. If you use a case outline like the one we recommend, you can start including references in the correct format from the start of your outline. While many find it slows down their writing as they stop to insert footnotes or endnotes and add sources to their reference list, our experience suggests it is a habit that is quickly learned and avoids a lot of difficult source searching later on. Anyone who has tried to go back to include the references after writing a case draft has learned the hard way that it is much better to include your sources as you write. Most secondary source cases will have several pages of sources for the case alone. We also strongly recommend that where possible, you download and archive copies of any reports, papers, media stories, and so on that you referenced in your case and IM/TN. This is important because if you have sourced these materials from an active website, the site could remove the information at a later date. It is frustrating when you try to go back to the source webpage (often during the review process), and you can no longer find the data. The bottom line is that when you choose to write a secondary source case, doing a lot of work on documenting your references is part of the job!

KEY CHAPTER TAKEAWAYS

- While most cases will include secondary data, there is a specific subsection of cases that are completely based on secondary data.
- Secondary source cases are a terrific way to write about an issue or company where you do not have access to a company contact, but where

data is available in other public realms. With a little creativity, aspiring case authors can craft a case story using only data collected from existing public sources.

- The appropriate sources will depend on your topic, but in particular we recommend sources such as company websites, traditional news media, social media (be careful!), books and scholarly articles, databases and market research data, and government records.
- A vital key to success in writing a secondary source case is to manage your sources properly. This means keeping accurate records of where – and when, for online sources – you found the information and how readers can access the same data.
- Sources are typically shown in a case in one of two formats: footnotes or endnotes. Find out from the start of your case which format your target outlet wants you to use and start doing so from your initial outline.
- Learn which citation system your target outlet prefers and use it from the start. This can usually be found in their information for authors.

Next, we discuss how to go about the actual case writing process.

7. The case writing process

Reaching the point where you are ready to start writing your case is a big step. It means you have (mostly) decided what kind of case you are writing (primary or secondary), what the case is about, and have completed much of the required research. Ideally, you have an outline of your case that maps out the main headings and key pieces of information that you need to convey. You probably have some ideas about the main elements of your case, such as who the main protagonist will be, where the story is situated, and the topic of the story. In fact, by the time you start to put your thoughts and research into narrative form, much of the story you want to tell will be in your head and itching to come out onto the page. At this stage in the case writing process, your choices about how you express and structure your narrative will greatly influence how effective your case ends up being. All the preparation work you have done to date – including deciding on your topics and collecting all your research – have laid the foundation for a great case.

It almost goes without saying that a great case must also be well-written to showcase that strong foundation. The way you choose to write your case can make or break how well your story works as a pedagogical tool; those using your case have to clearly understand and be interested in the context, the issue, the known and unknown information, and the decision-maker in order to learn effectively from the case. Cases that leave readers confused or bored result in frustration and disengagement. The purpose of this chapter is to help you learn how to tell your case story in a way that will maximize users' interest in and their ability to learn from your work. At the end of the day, remember that a case is a pedagogical tool for practising effective decision-making through vicarious experience.

For the sake of clarity, we have chosen to separate the chapters on the actual writing of the case and the writing of the instructor's manual or teaching note (IM/TN) (Chapter 8); however, the two documents are inextricably linked. Many authors recommend writing the two pieces simultaneously while others prefer to first complete the draft of the case and then follow with the IM/TN draft with iterative revisions to both until they are fully synchronized. As an author, you have to figure out whether the simultaneous or sequential approach works best for you, but either way be prepared for plenty of revisions, especially if your case undergoes peer review for a journal. We strongly recommend reading the next chapter (Chapter 8) on writing your IM/TN before starting to write your case so that you have a good understanding of the ways in which the two documents are related. While over time you will decide which approach works best for you, we will say that most experienced case writers we know write the two documents in parallel.

WHAT STORY ARE YOU TRYING TO TELL?

Writing a case is at its essence a form of storytelling. You are writing a story about an individual or group within the context of an organization who has to make a decision where there appear to be multiple valid choices, all of which have different anticipated future consequences that cannot be fully understood in advance. You want your readers to be able to see the issue from the perspective of the case protagonist so they can decide on the best course of action for that individual and for their organization.

Ensuring Appropriate Scope

Often one of the biggest challenges case writers have is deciding on one of many possible stories that they could tell about this organization or issue or person. Recall that a contemporary case is quite short – usually less than 10 pages of text. This means that focus is vital in case writing as authors simply do not have space to tell multiple stories. When gathering research, authors often find that there are several potential stories that could be told. Novice case writers will try to include data from several of these topics when developing their case, believing that it will result in a case with a broader appeal. However, experienced case writers understand that cases must be very highly focused on one key topic and storyline to link to theory effectively. In other words, case writers need to decide which story to tell and which one(s) to leave untold (which could become other fantastic cases). In addition to the length restriction of cases from publishers, the single case focus is also a requirement for the IM/TN as each case needs to target one particular discipline.

In our experience, the need to focus your case clearly on the one storyline that you have decided to tell is the most challenging part of learning effective case writing. It will mean that some of the data and research that you have collected will not be required and must be excluded from your case; that shouldn't be seen as a wasted effort but rather a sign of thorough researching. If you are struggling to get your case to the recommended page limit, go back again with a critical eye to make sure your nascent case is concentrated on that core topic. If you find your case is still too long, we recommend editing it one sentence at a time and deleting any sentences or words that are not absolutely required for the focused story you are telling. Be ruthless about this, removing any information, no matter how interesting, that is not directly connected to your core topic. Feedback from co-authors or colleagues can help with the editing process to make your case more focused (see section on obtaining feedback below) as they will review the case with a fresh pair of eyes and will be more willing to remove elements that do not fit the core narrative.

On the flip side, it is also important to have a substantial story with sufficient detail upon which to build a lesson. The scope of the case must be complex and detailed enough to prompt multiple perspectives and support meaningful classroom debate. Typically, new case authors tend towards having too wide a focus rather than too narrow. Learning how to hit the right balance between being too broad or too narrow as you write your case is a skill authors develop over time.

WHO IS TELLING THE STORY?

Having an Effective Protagonist

In deciding the specific focus for your story, you also need to decide from whose perspective the story is best told; that person then becomes your case protagonist who is tasked with making the core decision at the end of the case. Sometimes when you choose the topic focus the case protagonist becomes clear because there is only one possibility (e.g., the CEO). Other times, the case author has the choice of from whose perspective to tell the story because there are multiple viable options. For example, a case about whether a firm should pursue a carbon neutral strategy could be told from the perspective of the CEO making the final decision, or it could be told from the perspective of a COO trying to convince the CEO. Similarly, a case about the declining financial performance of a company could be made from the perspective of the CEO or it could be from the perspective of an external financial analyst deciding whether to recommend that his clients invest in the company. The correct choice for the author will depend on the actual case data as well as the learning objectives the author wishes to convey in the case.

As discussed in previous chapters, the choice of protagonist sometimes will depend on whether the case is a primary or secondary data case. In most primary data cases, your key contact (with whom you are working on the case) will be the obvious protagonist (e.g., Woodwark et al., 2020b), although we have written cases where it was actually the person to whom our contact reported who ended up being the case focus. The first thing that you need to obtain is the agreement from the individual to be featured as the protagonist in the case; if they have not been your main contact, it is a good idea to share with them a copy of a business case you have written (and have permission to share) so they can understand what it means to be featured as a protagonist in a case. The protagonist must in fact have decision-making authority about the main issue in the case and must be able to articulate the issue clearly. For readers to understand the context, the author should ensure the protagonist's role and responsibilities in the firm are clear. Organization charts are very helpful tools to communicate the organization's structure if authors can obtain one from the company or receive the company's permission to create one.

Cases are also a lot more interesting to readers when at least some personal details about the protagonist are shared, for example any hobbies, education background, past employers, and so on. Ideally, case authors can obtain this kind of information about their protagonists from company websites or social media (e.g., LinkedIn). Again, the advantage of primary data cases is that you can directly ask your protagonist contact for this information, which can sometimes unpackage interesting management preferences that make richer case data. Some case authors like to include photos or descriptions of their protagonists, although this is often only done if the protagonist's identity is deemed relevant to the case analysis. We recommend including any data about your protagonist that helps readers understand, analyse, and be interested in their story. Always ensure such information is included with the protagonist's approval.

TIMING FOR THE CASE

Date and Decision Time Frame

With rare exceptions, all cases take place in a specific moment in time when a decision must be made. The time of the case needs to be provided by authors early on, ideally in the introduction, as it grounds the rest of the information provided. Knowing the time frame should signal to the reader that certain courses of action were or were not possible at that time. For example, cases that are set in the early 1990s would not have solutions that involve social media or, even more broadly, the internet, as they were not yet prevalent (or even created).

The other important information related to timing is being specific about how long it is until the focal decision in the case must be made. This information is necessary because it can expand or constrict the set of options available to the protagonist. Authors often use this as a way to create a sense of urgency around the decision, and it is important to be clear about what is motivating or prompting a decision to be made about this issue now or in the immediate future. Ideally, authors have situated the case in time such that the pressure is mounting to decide, and the protagonist is strongly motivated to act in the immediate future. Be aware that for some publishing outlets the urgency issue is more important than for others, but most will want some indication that the focal decision is pressing.

Location

Authors must also situate the case in terms of the geographic location in which the protagonist is working and within which the focal decision will be made. While this should include the city and country, it is important to understand the broader impact of the decision: is it local, regional, at the provincial/state level, country level, or international? So, while the decision-maker could be sitting at their company headquarters in, for example, Cleveland, Ohio, the decision they are looking at could actually impact operations in a different state or country, depending on what they are considering. Knowing the location of both the organizational headquarters and the geographic location of the decision can help readers understand the context in which the firm operates, including factors such as national culture, political system, legal system, and so on. Decision-making is highly sensitive to such factors, so readers need to know where in the world the case is happening, typically down to the city level.

DECISION POINT

Recall that the case method is fundamentally a tool for teaching decision-making skills and that the most common type of case is the decision-based case. In a decision-based case, the key decision that the protagonist must take should be very clear to readers. While this sounds straightforward, it is often more challenging than it sounds because organizational decisions can be quite complex, in part because they are so sensitive to context. This means that in order to understand the key decision and its implications properly, readers must have a strong understanding of the organizational factors that influence the decision. Authors must clearly explain the context in which the focal decision is being made so they can choose the best course of action under the described specific set of circumstances as well as any articulated constraints.

When writing a case, sometimes authors find that the focal decision point is obvious from the start or becomes clear through the research process. Other times, case authors may have a choice of several potential decision points from which they could choose, each of which would lead to a different analysis and discussion. For example, multiple potential focal decisions can happen in primary data cases where there are several possible issues to discuss or with secondary data cases where the author has decided on a (popular) company rather than a specific incident or problem at the company. In such situations, authors must choose one option over the others as each case should only have one focal decision. Sometimes authors need to follow the lead of their case contact and protagonist as to which decision to select over other options. Other times, authors choose the decision that they think will most interest students or the decision that best supports the analysis they want to conduct in the IM/TN.

Finally, sometimes the focal decision is chosen based on data availability. The bottom line is that authors must anchor the case on one focal decision at a time and the analysis in the IM/TN revolves around that decision choice.

Multipart Cases

Cases that have multiple viable focal decisions do present authors with the opportunity to write a series of related cases or multipart cases (i.e., part A, part B, etc.). No doubt you have seen cases in this format where each part has a different stakeholder perspective or a new focal decision over time – sometimes even discussing the results from the previous decision – where the decisions are presented in chronological order (e.g., see Casciaro et al., 2005a; Casciaro et al., 2005b; Casciaro and Edmondson, 2007a; Casciaro and Edmondson, 2007b). This model can be a boon for the case author because often the result is from the same case research that has already been completed but the author gets to publish two or more related cases rather than just one.

The benefit for students is that they get feedback on their earlier decisions, which can enhance learning, and they also get to see how decisions within organizations are related to one another. Typically, multipart cases are used in classrooms such that the first part is assigned in advance, but subsequent parts are distributed in class or after the class discussion of part A. Hence, the part A case tends to be longer, and the part B or later cases tend to be shorter (often just a page) as much of the background information is already covered. The latter parts are often shorter by necessity so that they do not take up too much class time to read and absorb.

While authors often like multipart cases since they get more publications from their research and allow for a dynamic class discussion, they present challenges for case publishers and students. Multipart cases increase case package costs for students and can reduce case adoption rates since later parts typically do not stand alone. Sometimes it creates additional costs for the institution because it becomes the instructor's responsibility to provide the cases beyond the primary case, which are generally priced separately. If you are considering writing a multipart case, be sure to check with your target outlet in advance to see if they publish in that format. Textbook publishers and case distributors like Ivey Publishing may agree, but to our knowledge most journals will not. Increasingly, though, publishers are looking for subsequent cases that are also able to stand on their own rather than simply supplement a prior case.

CASE FORMAT

Much like a research paper, the traditional format for a case follows a predictable structure: introduction; body; and conclusion with optional exhibits and references.

Structure

The introduction is arguably the most important section of your case because it summarizes the situation and motivates the reader to proceed. It is typically one page or less, consisting of two or three paragraphs. In the introduction, authors need to include all the key components for the full story that will unfold throughout the rest of the case narrative. In short, the introduction is like a synopsis in terms of content where the reader learns the key information in the case such as the focal organization, the protagonist, the time and location of the case, the focal decision to be made, and why a decision must be made now. However, the introduction also needs to capture the interest of readers so that they want to learn more. One way to do this is to foreshadow some of the information and challenges in the case that will be unpackaged as the case develops; effective introductions are a great place to put direct quotations that hint at the case conflict. Be mindful of the fact that time-strapped students may only read the introduction before class and so it has to provide an excellent overview. Beyond students, instructors looking to add your course to their class may also only read the first paragraph to get a sense of its relevance and appeal, which is another reason to make your introduction as engaging as possible!

The next section of the case is the main body, which is where the majority of the supplementary case data is located. The start of this section is usually signalled by a new heading. There are different ways to organize the data in the body of the case. Some authors like to start the body with the big picture level after the introduction by outlining the industry level information. Other authors like to follow the introduction with a detailed section about the case company, the case protagonist, or the main issue at hand. There are many effective ways to organize your case data, so you just need to determine how the information flows best for each case you write, based on the level of analysis you have selected. The use of headings throughout the body of the case narrative helps guide the reader (usually students) to find specific information as they think through the case analysis. It also helps to break up the volume of text on a page to make it more readable.

By the time you have finished crafting the body of the case, all the information required to analyse the case should be included, unless the information will be covered later in exhibits. Some technical cases or ones where a lot of history is required to understand the situation can have very long body sections of six or more pages. However, for a short case, the body section may be only two or three pages. Remember that all the data needed to conduct the analysis you outline in your IM/TN must be included in the case since students do not get access to the IM/TN. A common novice error is to include data in the IM/TN that is not included in the case, but which is needed for the analysis (we will talk more about that in Chapter 8). Make sure to double check that all the data you need for the analysis can be found in the body and exhibits.

The last section in a case is the conclusion, which creatively summarizes the overall situation and decision facing the case protagonist. The conclusion should not introduce any new data, but rather should briefly review the key decision being addressed in the case. In that sense, the conclusion is not unlike an abstract of a research paper but written in an engaging tone instead of a neutral one. Remember that the conclusion, like the introduction, is important because it is likely to be the last part of the case students will read before the class discussion. The conclusion should leave students interested in doing the analysis and having an active discussion in the classroom. Be sure that all the information in the conclusion is consistent with what is in the introduction, although rephrased rather than a direct repeat. Authors should aim for the conclusion section to be less than one page of typically no more than two paragraphs. As in introductions, quotations can be effective in this section. If you are using endnotes rather than footnotes, the endnote section typically follows on a new page after the conclusion.

Some cases will include a section of exhibits where authors can provide detailed data that would be too much for the case body. Often financial data is reported this way, or illustrations and photos. If you do not need an exhibit for your case, you do not have to include any; however, exhibits can be a more efficient and compelling way to present data that will be important for the case analysis. This is becoming increasingly important as case publishers are looking to shorten the case narrative section of cases. Remember though, only include information that is necessary for the case analysis – the need-to-have rather than the nice-to-have. All exhibits must also recognize their source, even if they have been created by the case authors.

The last section in a case is the reference section. For a secondary case, this section will be quite long, usually with multiple pages. But even a primary source case will often have many secondary sources that need to be included as references. Previous chapters have already covered the importance of being robust in your referencing in the case and IM/TN and having a system in place for referencing before you even start writing your case.

CASE WRITING CONVENTIONS

The activity of case writing has developed some standard conventions over time that are now widely accepted and therefore expected practices. These conventions relate to writing tense, writing tone, and including balanced or all-inclusive information.

Tense

One of the strangest conventions that new case writers have to get used to is that cases are always written in the past tense. Although case writers may have read dozens of cases, they may not ever have noticed that this is the way cases are written. Typically, the organization one is writing about is still a going concern that not only continues to exist, but that you expect will continue to exist for many years to come. Authors therefore struggle to write about the firm and protagonist in the past tense throughout the case. Although using the past tense is mostly a practice of convention, the rationale is that authors are describing a specific scenario that existed at a point in time necessarily in the past. The main exception to the past tense rule is that when using direct quotations, the quotation should stay in the original tense and use the exact language. The use of the past tense in case writing is occasionally debated at case conferences, but to our knowledge it is universally accepted as the expected style and unlikely to ever change. In fact, some case journals are explicit that if they receive a case that has not been written in the past tense, it will be returned without review (e.g., see author guidelines at *The CASE Journal* at Emerald Publishing Group). Even for live cases where the situation being described is currently on-going and unresolved, the case should be written in the past tense. This is a great example of why having your case peer reviewed by a colleague is such a good idea as it is very easy (even for experienced case writers) to slip up and accidentally use the present tense when writing the case.

Neutral Tone

Another expectation for case writing style is that the information in the case be conveyed in a neutral tone as opposed to a positive or supportive tone, or a negative unsupportive tone. This is because it is not the case author's job to evaluate anything depicted in the case but rather to report the facts in a neutral manner, much as a reporter would in a news story. Case authors should not opine in the case document so as not to bias readers, although they are free to do so in the IM/TN document to which only instructors have access. If you present information or opinion that is inaccurate, unsubstantiated, or emotive about your protagonist or organization, the case publisher could ask you to remove the information or reject the case for publication. Ensuring your case has a neutral, unbiased tone, and contains accurate, substantiated information helps protect both you and the case publisher from defamation and libel suits from the organization. Again, this is another area where a friendly reviewer can be helpful as it is easy not to spot the biases in our own writing.

Self-contained Information

A final expectation of case writers is to remember that all of the information required for the case analysis should be provided in the case or the case exhibits. As we pointed out previously in this chapter, in conventional case analysis students are asked not to go outside the case for additional information and insight. The fact that all the required data to analyse the case must be contained within it is one of the reasons why it is so important to develop the case in conjunction with the IM/TN (which we explore in Chapter 8). The case questions you will develop in the IM/TN should be directly linked to the information you provide in the case narrative and exhibits so that students are able to perform a robust analysis linked to the theoretical underpinnings of the case.

Use of Quotations

Direct quotations from your case protagonist and other supporting actors are often used in case writing and typically encouraged by reviewers and editors. Make sure they are accurate and approved by the person to whom they are attributed. Judicious use of quotations can bring the case narrative to life and can help convey the personalities of the case characters. Quotations can come from either primary sources through interviews or cited from secondary sources with proper attribution. Recall that when using existing quotations, the original tense is retained.

MANAGING THE WRITING PROCESS

Obtaining Feedback

Remember that as a case author, at the end of the writing process you need to be able to meet two important goals. First, if you are writing a primary source case, you will need to obtain sign-off from your key contact to formally release the case for use. Second, you are likely to want your case to be published (in a case journal, through a case publisher, and/or in a textbook) or accepted at a conference. In order to meet both goals, we strongly recommend getting plenty of feedback on your draft case and IM/TN as they are developed.

Specifically, there are three main stages of development where we think it is critical to get feedback on your case: upon completion of the draft introduction; the draft body; and the draft conclusion.

If you are writing a primary source case, your most important provider of feedback at these three stages is of course your key contact – the person who will eventually release your case. We recommend asking for feedback in writing at each of these three stages so that any concerns can be addressed upfront, and so that your contact builds confidence in you and commitment to the final outcome.

When asking your contact for feedback, make sure they understand that your goal is to represent them and their story in a way they are fully comfortable with. Show them that you are willing to make changes as requested, particularly if it is to change something that is factually incorrect. Make suggested changes promptly upon receipt and ensure the changes meet your contact's expectations. In the event that you cannot make a particular change, explain why not and negotiate an alternative that works for both of you. We recommend completing the revisions to each section before moving on to later parts of your case. Repeat the feedback process for each major stage of the case development until the case is ready to be released. We further recommend keeping copies of the drafts of your case, noting the changes made, in case there are any questions later on about why they were done. This can be helpful if the personnel at your focal company change (which can happen if the case is taking a while to write) and they question why certain case writing decisions were taken.

While this chapter solely deals with writing the case, a pro tip is to make sure your IM/TN is well-developed before you ask for final release on the case. That way, you can be certain that the data you need to meet the case learning objectives is complete in the case (more about this next in Chapter 8). Lastly, if you are trying to publish your primary source case in a peer-reviewed journal, make sure your contact understands that the case release is for the initial submission but that the review process will lead to further revisions, which will also require approval at a later stage. Always keep your contact appraised of the status of the project as the writing process proceeds.

If you are writing a secondary source case, you do not need to worry about the case release; nevertheless, we recommend getting feedback at the same three stages of the draft development. Some authors choose co-authors to fulfil this role which can be a great strategy. Others use colleagues and eventually even students when testing the case (see Chapter 9). Whoever you choose to provide feedback on your case as it develops, do ensure you get multiple rounds of feedback along the way and revise accordingly.

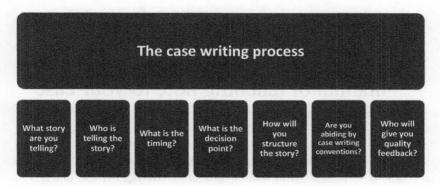

Figure 7.1   The case writing process

KEY CHAPTER TAKEAWAYS

- Writing up your case is a chance to showcase all your research and work to date. It's also when your case starts to come to life and an author starts to see what it will be like to eventually use the case in the classroom.
- Early on, case authors must determine which story they wish to tell and ensure it is focused on one main topic while still having enough depth for discussion.
- In the case introduction, authors must communicate the full context of the case including the identity of the protagonist, the time frame and location of the case, and the main case decision point. The body of the case includes all the background data to understand the case context and issue, and the conclusion reiterates the focal decision and its implications.
- Be sure to follow the case writing conventions including writing only in the past tense, using a neutral tone, providing balanced information, and using quotations where possible.
- Authors should seek out regular feedback as the case narrative develops to improve clarity and understanding.

In Chapter 8 we will walk you through the steps of drafting your IM/TN and provide all the tips and tricks we know to help you be successful in that vital stage.

8.   Writing the accompanying instructor's manual or teaching note to your case

With all the work you have put into your case so far, it is time to focus on developing the accompanying instructor's manual (IM), also called the teaching note (TN). The appropriate term depends on the outlet in which you are looking to publish, with some publishers preferring IM and others TN. Regardless of the term used by your target outlet, the required content of the IM/TN will be similar in many ways but each outlet will have a unique style authors must follow. In this chapter, we will cover all the IM/TN elements of which we are aware although for any one outlet, only some of these will be required. Again, be sure to find out in advance what the current required content, style, and format are for the IM/TN at your target outlet as each publisher uses somewhat different terminology, section headings, and order.

Most users of cases are more familiar with the case document than the IM/TN document since only the case is openly published. However, many in the case research community believe that the bulk of the intellectual contribution of any case resides in the IM/TN. Clearly, the IM/TN is not intended to be a stand-alone document, so really this attitude reflects the fact that cases are necessarily designed to be used in combination with the accompanying IM/TN. It is in the joint development and use of a case and IM/TN that make an academic contribution to the field within which they are written. The fact that the IM/TN is essential to any case author's contribution can be a surprise to some authors since most users of the case will never (hopefully) lay eyes on the IM/TN as they are supposed to be limited in access only to confirmed instructors. For the purpose of authors demonstrating their impact and contribution in their field (i.e., for tenure and promotion applications), we strongly recommend that authors always provide a copy of each IM/TN to accompany each case they have written. The complete set of case and IM/TN makes a much stronger illustration of the impact of your work than simply relying on the publicly distributed documents.

The IM/TN is where authors demonstrate how to relate the specifics of each individual case to the general principles of a discipline. Hence, the process of developing an IM/TN is an inductive reasoning process where the author moves from the specifics of the case to the general linkages and conclusions within a disciplinary field. Case authors must learn how to take the specifics of a case and relate them to the broader lessons from the research literature on that topic. The key intellectual contribution in case research comes from rigorously examining the relationship between the specific details in the case to the related literature for the chosen disciplinary perspective and from examining how the case specifics help case users to better understand the applicable research findings. Some cases are designed to illustrate what the literature would expect to happen in practice, while other cases are designed to illustrate exceptions to what the literature would predict. Thus, cases and IM/TNs are at the intersection between inductive and deductive reasoning, and at the intersection of research and practice. While many scholars who do not do case research assume it is easier to do case research than other forms of research, we believe that it is a unique skill-set in and of itself that makes a singular contribution to the business and management disciplines.

HOW IM/TN IS USED BY CASE INSTRUCTORS

Unlike the case, which has both students and instructors as users, the IM/TN is intended to be used only by instructors. Publishers go to great lengths to try to ensure that remains true by validating teaching credentials prior to access; however, the reality is there are many IM/TNs available on the internet through paid case solution sites for those students who choose to seek them out. While this is something to be mindful of as a case instructor, we nevertheless recommend making your IM/TN complete and thorough as it is a tool to help your case-teaching peers be successful in getting the most out of the case from a learning perspective. Over time, it is inevitable that the IM/TN for a popular case will become available outside the authorized access, but one of the drivers of case popularity is the quality of the IM/TN which encourages instructors to adopt a case in the first place. Just be aware that IM/TN security is never perfect.

The two main uses of an IM/TN for instructors are for case selection and class preparation. While new authors may not realize this, the IM/TN is probably the most significant resource in terms of case selection. While factors like case topic and length matter, most instructors choose cases based on the learning objectives (LOs) they would like to achieve and topics they would like to cover in their course. To find out whether a particular case will meet their needs, many instructors will review the first page or two of the IM/TN to read the synopsis, the LOs, and the target course. It is worth highlighting that if your case is being distributed through a case publisher, they will often have a search function on their website that allows you to search for cases linked to broad subject categories (e.g., marketing, operations, or accounting) to narrow the search from the thousands of cases they have on offer. A search can then be further refined by looking for topic areas within those subjects, so again, as you develop your IM/TN it is important that you know the subject area in which you would like your case to reside and its core theoretical focus to make it more accessible to searchers on the site. As such, one of the functions of the first few pages of the IM/TN is to communicate to instructors what your case is all about (highlighting the subject and topic area), what students will learn from using it, and why it will create interesting class engagement.

The other major use of the IM/TN is for detailed class preparation. When most instructors use a case for the first time, they rely quite heavily on the IM/TN to prepare for the case discussion. Instructors who assign case preparation questions in advance of class may well use the suggested assignment questions from the IM/TN exactly as written the first time through to see how the class works from a timing and discussion perspective. This allows the instructor to follow the suggested teaching plan in the IM/TN very closely for the first use. It is important to remember that most instructors will not have read the entire IM/TN in detail until they need to prepare for class, so make sure your entire IM/TN is consistent with the description you provided about what would be covered and that the quality of the work and analysis in the IM/TN is high. A strong IM/TN is more likely to lead to a successful first class with a new case and therefore much more likely to subsequently be used again by that instructor. Strong IM/TNs lead to both case adoption, case classroom success, and case re-adoption. Arguably, your IM/TN is as important if not more important than your case. As you will see from the rest of the discussion in this chapter, the IM/TN is often the most challenging and time-consuming part of the case research process too.

One rule to know about drafting your IM/TN that will save you time and hassle is that the IM/TN should never have added information about the case that is not in the case itself. In other words, case information required for the analysis of questions proposed in the IM/TN must actually be included in the case rather than in the proposed answers to the questions. While this may seem so obvious that it does not need to be said, it is very easy for authors to accidentally use information in the IM/TN that may have been edited out of the current case version, or that they know about and think is included in the case when in fact it is not. Case authors have a lot of information in their heads while they write, and it is easy to lose track of which data has and has not been included in the story. Hence, we strongly recommend having your case reviewed by a friendly colleague or tested in a classroom before you submit your case for publication to ensure that the IM/TN is robust enough to support the in-class experience. It is worth noting that an exception to this rule is any epilogue you include in the IM/TN related to what actually happened after the decision-timing in the case.

While new data should not be introduced in the case, that does not mean that the IM/TN should just repeat those case facts. One of the biggest complaints about IM/TNs results from them not including the analysis prompted by the case questions. For example, if you ask students to conduct a financial analysis of the annual performance of a company, all of that analysis should be included as an exhibit in the teaching note; you do not (and should not) include the actual financial analysis in the case itself as it is part of the work students should complete to understand what has happened and to help them answer the decision question. In a strategic management course, if you ask students to perform an analysis of the external environment (e.g., PEST or Porter's Five Forces frameworks), the exhibits in the IM/TN should include completed versions of those tools. This is important as individuals teaching your case may be teaching it last minute and may not have time to complete the analysis on their own prior to class. The inclusion of the academic analysis to support the case is a critical piece of the IM/TN and will help with its adoption by instructors.

DISCUSSION OF IM/TN FORMAT RELATED TO PUBLICATION TARGET

While the format for cases is similar across publishers, the format for the IM/TN varies substantially by publishing outlet. As we have said before (and will say again in later chapters), it is vital to determine in advance the required format for the outlet you are targeting. If you do not follow the requested format, authors risk their case being desk rejected by editors for being incomplete, or risk receiving unfavourable reviews and commentary from reviewers. Do everyone a favour and tailor your IM/TN to the outlet where you intend to submit your case each and every time. While you may have a preferred format for your IM/TN, publishers want them to be consistent in the categories included and so require specific elements in a specific order. So, while you may think you are improving on their format by including additional sections, it is unlikely that your variations on the required format will stand, and you will have wasted your time (and irritated the reviewers and publishing team). Keep it simple and follow the instructions in detail.

KEY IM/TN ELEMENTS

The following list of IM/TN elements is compiled from a range of case journals and publishers in order to provide the breadth of sections that you could be asked to include in an IM/TN. It will be rare that all of these elements will be required in any one IM/TN, but if you submit cases to a range of publishing outlets, you will be likely to encounter all of them at some point. We have put them in the order in which they most commonly appear in the IM/TN. Remember that with the exception of the suggested discussion questions which might be shared with students in advance, the audience for the IM/TN is only instructors.

Synopsis or Abstract

The synopsis or abstract is a brief summary of the case and is always the first section in any IM/TN. This section lets instructors know what the case is about at a high level so they can decide quickly whether or not this case is a fit for their needs and will be interesting for the intended students. The synopsis should describe the case organization and context, the case protagonist's perspective, and the focal decision that will be considered in the case. Some outlets will include the target courses for which the case is designed as well as a concise summary of the case LOs. Other outlets will only include the case summary information, relying instead on the subsequent two sections (LOs and course target and usage) to round out an instructor's understanding of the case. The synopsis is only printed in the IM/TN (not the case itself) but is also reprinted on the case website for the case journal, case publisher, or case distributer.

Learning Objectives (LOs)

In this section, the author outlines for instructors what the case is designed to teach the students who study it – the learning objectives, or 'LOs'. For most new case authors, this section is the most challenging because it requires authors to clearly articulate the purpose and value of the case from a learner's perspective. Best practice for the LO section is to state the objectives in terms of what students will be able to do after completing the case analysis. For example, a case in strategic management where students are learning Porter's Five Forces model might state that after studying this case students will be able to apply Porter's Five Forces model to the focal case industry. A case about equity theory in organizational behaviour might list a LO that states that students will be able to apply the concepts of equity theory to the case situation and predict the potential reactions to inequity. LOs should be numbered and typically range from three to five maximum. If there are more than five LOs, that usually means there is not enough focus to the IM/TN.

The LO section is one of the most important – if not the most important – section in the IM/TN. It is the section where the author articulates why the case is important for students to experience and that convinces instructors that it will deliver learning consistent with what the instructor intends, and judges appropriate for his or her students. During the review process, the LO section is almost always an area that reviewers ask authors to develop and revise. What is often difficult for new authors to understand is that the core elements of a written case can be used for quite different purposes by different instructors depending on their respective perspectives. The LO section of the IM/TN demands that authors clearly articulate their intended purpose for the case, recognizing that there are always other possible LOs that could have been selected. During the review process, reviewers will accept some LOs and suggest others for authors to consider. Some of the most common feedback on this section is that the authors need to think more clearly and more specifically about the student learning that will stem from the case. Other common feedback is that the data in the case is not sufficient or does not align with the stated learning outcomes, in which case either the case data or the IM/TN LOs need to be revised to bring them into alignment.

The bottom line is that thinking deeply about the intended LOs is an important first step before tackling the rest of the IM/TN. It anchors the IM/TN and provides the rationale and motivation for the connection to the case data. Most experienced case authors will develop this section simultaneously while they write the case so that they are actively thinking through the LOs while the case narrative is being crafted. We recommend at least drafting an initial set of LOs during early case writing to keep them top of mind throughout the process. Be sure to revisit them whenever you revise the case to ensure they continually remain aligned. Best practice is to indicate the corresponding LO number throughout the IM/TN sections so instructors can clearly see how each section maps to the overall case LOs. For instance, each discussion question and each topic in the theory, concepts, and framework sections should clearly indicate which LO is being covered. This is helpful to instructors because sometimes they need to truncate or adapt the teaching plan to cover only some of the LOs. Labelling the LOs that are being covered throughout the IM/TN sections allows the logic behind the IM/TN components to be transparent.

Course Target, Student Level, and Usage

This section outlines for instructors how the author has designed the case to be used. It should include a list of appropriate course discipline(s) that the case targets, as well as the intended student level, and where in the course it is likely to fit best. One of the most common comments by reviewers is that case authors are overly optimistic about their case appeal, particularly where the case author suggests the case could be used in multiple course disciplines. While there are multi-disciplinary cases (which are a specific type of case and complex to write), a good case and IM/TN should be targeted to a single topic in a single discipline. This makes them effective classroom tools because they are purpose-designed for that LO (as noted in the strategic management and organizational behaviour LO examples in the previous section).

You also need to think about the most appropriate student level for your case; executive students with years of work experience bring different knowledge to case analysis than first-year undergraduate students. As such, some case topics are more appropriate for one student level than another and it is in this section that you will need to be clear who will most benefit from your case. There are cases that can be used across multiple target student levels and exceptional IM/TNs will outline how the in-class discussion may differ depending on the student level selected. Finally, a case could be a good warm-up or review case to be used early on in the course, a mid-course case that assumes some prior knowledge, or a summary or capstone case that covers topics usually covered towards the end of a course. A case could also be listed as a good exam or assignment case. The idea here is for the author to suggest to the instructors who are looking at adopting the case how the author believes it can be used most effectively. Of course, the final decision is the instructors' as they can choose to use the case for whatever course, student level, or course placement they wish. In this section, authors may also wish to include the length of class time for which the case and IM/TN was designed (usually 60 or 90 minutes) although the timing should also be included in the case teaching plan (outlined below).

Case Methodology

The case methodology section is where the author describes how the case data was collected. If the case is from primary data, the author should disclose how the data was obtained (e.g., through in-person, online, or telephone interviews with the protagonist or other individuals) and the period over which the interviews took place. If the case was written purely using secondary sources only, the author should disclose that clearly. Other sources such as podcasts or books should also be disclosed. Any relationship between the case authors and the case organization should be disclosed here, particularly if the case is based on personal experience or if there was a financial incentive provided by the company to create the case. This section may also include information regarding whether the case has been tested in the classroom or used as part of an internal or external case competition.

Theory, Concepts, and/or Frameworks

This section in the IM/TN goes by different names and is only required by certain outlets, primarily peer-reviewed case journals. The purpose of this section is to outline the theory, concepts, and/or frameworks that the case is designed to teach. This section should align closely with the LO section. For example, if LO#1 is that students will be able to apply equity theory to the focal organization and predict response to inequity, then the author should provide a summary of equity theory and responses to inequity from the literature. In other words, this section outlines the literature that instructors need to know in order to teach the case and ensure the LOs are met. Typically, each theory, concept, or framework will have a heading and LO number followed by a summary paragraph, or several if required, along with applicable sourcing. Some cases will have only one major theory, concept, or framework, while others will have several included in the same case. Publishing outlets that require this section argue that it helps to make the connection between the unique case situation described in the case narrative and the broader disciplinary literature the case is being used to teach. Such outlets contend that making this connection explicit in each published case is the most rigorous form of case research and the standard to which the form should be held. In addition, it provides important background for instructors who may not have a deep understanding of that theory or framework and are required to teach the case as part of a coordinated course. One expert tip is to align the topics in this section with the LOs you have laid out above and then label each topic with the specific LO number to which is relates, so it is clear to instructors what the relationship is between LOs and theory.

Academic Resources for Instructors

This section provides instructors with suggested resources to learn more about the topics covered in the case, as well as potential resources for use in class. Examples of the types of resources included in this section are textbooks noting the specific chapters covering the topic being covered, journal articles, relevant videos such as TED talks, or even podcasts. Some outlets simply require a list of these resources along with complete referencing. Other outlets request a short annotation for each resource including how the instructor could best use the resource. For example, in the annotated section the author suggests which student level each resource would be appropriate for if the instructor wished to assign it in conjunction with the case as a background reading, as an in-class handout, or an in-class exercise. The overall idea here is that this section allows instructors to prepare for the class easily where they use the case without having to do any further research beyond the IM/TN. Try to keep the resources outlined in this section as available as possible; not all academic institutions have the same access to materials and journal subscriptions. Luckily, one of the marks of a great IM/TN is that all the preparation and research that case instructors need to do in order to be ready to teach the case has already been done. Not all instructors will use all the resources provided, but if they wish to avail themselves of such supporting resources they do not have to look beyond the IM/TN. Remember that the internet (e.g., the company's website, YouTube) can be a great resource as you write this section, particularly for engaging content that can capture your students' attention as you begin the case discussion.

Discussion Questions and Answers

This is one of the most recognized sections of the IM/TN, providing a set of suggested discussion questions to be assigned to students. It is also typically one of the longest sections in the IM/TN. The best practice is first to list the set of questions on their own (i.e., without the answers), and then to repeat the questions followed by the suggested answers and analysis. This customary practice is done so instructors can easily copy and paste just the questions when assigning them to students. The number of suggested discussion questions can vary from about three to eight, but most authors include between four and six questions. We would only recommend a higher number of questions if you were writing the case to be delivered over multiple classes or a longer teaching block (e.g., three hours). One tip is to align your discussion questions with the LO section (outlined above) and label each question with a specific LO number so the alignment between the two sections is clear. This can be helpful for instructors who choose to pursue only some of the suggested LOs in the case and need to know how to streamline the other sections including the discussion questions to include only the selected ones. Widespread practice is to include one introductory or warm-up question to launch the case, and one final question that asks students to decide, along with a detailed rationale, on the key decision question the protagonist is considering.

After listing the suggested questions, authors provide a robust answer for each one. In their answers, authors include a combination of case data and theory, concepts, or frameworks that they want students to apply in their answers. Remember that no new case data should be introduced in the answers; all case data must already be in the case so that students have access to it. The answers to questions should thoroughly analyse the case data in relation to the relevant theory. When answering questions, the best IM/TNs provide specific examples of the type of answers they expect according to student level. For example, the first part of the answer is how the instructor should expect most undergraduate students to be able to respond, while the second part of the suggested answer specifies how stronger students could respond or how graduate-level students might respond. In general, the suggested answer for each question typically runs about one page long, although it can run quite a bit longer. Hence, this section usually runs between four and eight – or even more – pages long. While this may seem like overkill, the intent is to prepare the instructor thoroughly for the range of student answers that could come up in class and for the complete analysis he or she wishes students to be able to conduct. All of the analysis expected from the students should be provided by the author; if the discussion question asks for a PEST analysis, that analysis should be included either in the body of the answer or as an IM/TN case exhibit.

Case Teaching Plan

This important section is where authors present a complete suggested teaching plan for how to use the case in class including how much time to devote to each step. Typically, authors suggest an introduction to the case which serves as a warm-up for the class discussion for the first five to 10 minutes. Sometimes this is a fun discussion about the case company or topic, a video introducing the students to a new company, or a discussion about the level of experience the class has with the type of challenge in the case. It is really up to the author to propose an engaging introduction into the case discussion, but instructors can of course choose whether the suggestion will work for their students. Next, authors often propose launching into the case analysis directly by starting with the easiest (and usually first) discussion question. The rest of the discussion questions can follow in the teaching plan (along with suggested timing for each), and sometimes there are exercises or videos interspersed. Authors can propose that students work in groups to decide on a joint response to a question, or to work with the full class. It is worth noting that while most teaching plans are aligned with the discussion questions, some teaching plans will incorporate additional elements to keep the students on their toes. Authors can propose activities like debates, votes, or role-plays to help bring the focal issues to life and to work through the case analysis. While it is always fun to include class group work for them to discuss the questions, it is helpful to include a version that does not include class group work in case the class size is too large for that to be an effective strategy. For a more detailed review of case teaching plans, we recommend Erskine et al. (2003).

Your teaching plan should be aligned with the case LOs, with sufficient time devoted to the most important LOs. Typically, teaching plans end with a summary of the issue and a recommendation with rationale for the case protagonist. If the case has an epilogue, instructors can spend the last few minutes of class advising students what actually happened, including the real decision made and any outcomes that resulted from that. With any remaining class time, instructors can discuss the class's response to the epilogue and their takeaway lessons from the case. A great case teaching plan can help instructors new to the case to quickly develop a lesson plan for the class that is suited to the needs of each class. Together with the timing cues, the teaching plan can help an instructor know if he or she is on track during the class session, so they do not run out of time to complete the analysis. This can be presented as a table, breaking down the core case analysis sections, along with the proposed timing cues for each.

Online Teaching Plan

Increasingly, publishers are asking authors to include a section in their IM/TN specifically about how to teach the case online – either synchronously or asynchronously. Sometimes little about the teaching plan discussed above needs to change to teach a case online, but other times there are required changes to how the case is presented, or there may also be new opportunities available for online use of the case (e.g., Zoom polls, breakout rooms, chat or discussion boards, etc.). Even if your publisher does not require a separate section about online teaching, we do recommend including a brief section in your IM/TN for instructors who are considering using your case in online classes. Be sure to consider both synchronous and asynchronous online teaching plans; asynchronous delivery of cases requires additional insight and guidance in terms of how interactive case discussions can be sequenced over hours or days.

Exhibits and Appendices

One of the final (and most important) sections in your IM/TN is for any exhibits or appendices that you wish to include to support your case analysis. These components can be graphics or visuals that instructors can use in class. They can also be charts, graphs, tables, or figures which contain case analysis. As noted earlier, if your discussion questions for students involve specific types of analysis, then it is critical that you include the completed analysis in your IM/TN and the appropriate place is often in the exhibit section. Another popular exhibit is suggested board plans for right, left, and centre or top and bottom boards; this is required by some publishers. These are incredibly helpful for instructors teaching your case for the first time as it allows them to see the progression through the case analysis. While many instructors will not actually have classrooms with multiple boards, these exhibits can be reproduced in slides or handouts instead. Some IM/TNs have few exhibits besides what is required by the publisher, while others have several, particularly if there are photos or graphics as part of the case analysis. For example, a marketing case about choosing branding and logo options might include a few pages of graphics which the instructor can use in class. Note that when exhibits and appendices in the IM/TN are numbered they are called exhibit IM/TN 1, or IM/TN appendix 1, to differentiate them from the exhibits or appendices in the case document.

Epilogue (If Available)

Many students and instructors really enjoy finding out at the end of a case discussion what actually happened in the case. The purpose of the epilogue section in the IM/TN is to let students know what happened after the end of the case timeline so they can compare their recommended decision to the actual decision. Ideally, the case author can also provide insight into the outcome of the actual decision. Instructors can augment their case discussion by comparing the class's decision-making to the actual decision and speculate about how the outcomes would compare. It is important to remind the class that even though the company may have taken a specific decision, it does not necessarily mean that it was the best decision. This helps to ensure that students who may have made a different recommendation do not feel that their solution was necessarily 'wrong'.

References

This section is straightforward – it is simply a list of all the sources used in the IM/TN. Most of the resources in the IM/TN will be academic sources such as journal articles or textbooks. If your case is a secondary source case, many of your case sources will also appear in the IM/TN reference list. A good reference list makes it easy for instructors to find the resources you recommend in the IM/TN, as well as the ones you relied on for your case analysis. Be sure to check the citation format required by your publishing outlet.

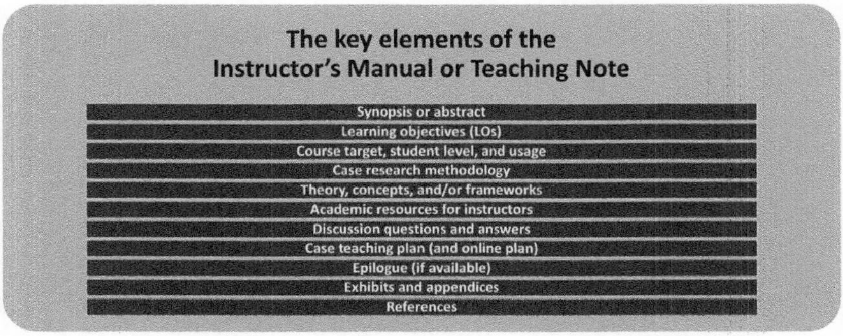

The key elements of the Instructor's Manual or Teaching Note

- Synopsis or abstract
- Learning objectives (LOs)
- Course target, student level, and usage
- Case research methodology
- Theory, concepts, and/or frameworks
- Academic resources for instructors
- Discussion questions and answers
- Case teaching plan (and online plan)
- Epilogue (if available)
- Exhibits and appendices
- References

Figure 8.1   Key elements of the instructor's manual or teaching note

KEY CHAPTER TAKEAWAYS

- Writing the IM/TN is often the most challenging part of learning to be a case researcher. In our experience, the more of them you write, the easier the process will become. Being a case reviewer will also help you improve your skills.
- Remember that the IM/TN is where unique case stories become connected to the broader disciplinary theory and literature and also how students learn to glean generalizable lessons from the specific situation they have studied.
- The IM/TN is the heart of each case and represents the crux of the contribution it makes. Excellent IM/TN writing is therefore critical for your cases to have maximum impact.
- It is also important to remember that IM/TNs are simply suggestions about how instructors could choose to use your case. Each instructor is always free to use your case however he or she sees fit for each scenario.

In Chapter 9 we will discuss having your case and IM/TN friendly peer reviewed by a colleague and testing your case with students prior to submission for publication.

9. Testing your case

When you have completed a full draft of your case and your instructor's manual or teaching note (IM/TN), and ideally you have received at least some peer feedback on it already, you are ready to test your case. Testing your case means at a minimum trying it out for the first time with a class and then revising as necessary based on what you learned. While this may sound like an optional step, it is increasingly becoming a requirement for peer-reviewed cases. Reviewers and editors strongly suggest that authors classroom test their case and then revise it in response to student and peer feedback prior to submission.[1]

We support this approach and believe case authors should make testing new cases a regular part of their pre-publication process; there is no better way to make sure the core elements are coming out in the class discussion and that your case has both the flow and timing that you have intended. Yes, it is an additional step to complete prior to publication. But, if it increases reviewer and editor confidence in your work, testing your case in advance before the review process rather than during a time-constrained review period could save you time in the end and increase the likelihood that your case will be accepted for publication. Ultimately, by the time you are done testing your case you should feel that another instructor (who did not write the case like you did) would be able to teach the case effectively by relying solely on what has been included in the case and IM/TN.

WHAT TO DO WHEN YOU HAVE A FULL CASE AND IM/TN DRAFTED

Once you have a completed draft of your case and IM/TN that you feel is ready for feedback, we recommend you start with getting initial input via either a friendly peer review or via a case conference (ideally both). The former is a flexible process where you can get feedback quickly, while the latter is less flexible timing wise but can provide helpful feedback from multiple case writing experts, particularly if authors are looking to publish their case in a particular outlet. Several outlets provide author checklists to help ensure they have included all the requirements and have avoided common mistakes.[2] We note that some outlets suggest first testing the case in class, revising it, and then obtaining a final round of peer feedback. This approach could work well too, but in our experience, we prefer to obtain peer review first, followed by in-class testing, and then make a final set of revisions because we want the first in-class test to be as strong as possible. It is up to you as the author to decide which order of feedback makes the most sense for your case.

PEER REVIEW

Friendly Peer Review

The first place to start is with a friendly review from a trusted colleague, ideally one who writes cases or is otherwise familiar with case research. The idea of a friendly peer review is for your colleague to identify issues in advance of submission and to provide any other feedback on how your case and IM/TN can be improved before you submit it for publication. This is of course a service you will offer in return for his or her cases so you can each benefit from the exchange. Ideally, your peer review is from a colleague in your field who knows the topics you are covering in your IM/TN so their practical and theory expertise can be leveraged to develop your work. However, if that is not possible, a colleague in another discipline who has experience writing cases can still be quite helpful and much preferable to no peer review. While we put a lot of effort and focus into our work as writers, it is easy to become too close to our work to review or edit it effectively. The other great thing about working with a peer on friendly reviews is that you may end up with a great new co-author from the process if you find he or she is interested and provides a lot of value to your materials.

When asking a peer to do a friendly review, here are some suggestions or reminders about the characteristics to consider for the case and the IM/TN.

Case
- Is the case well-written using case writing conventions (e.g., proper spelling and grammar, past tense)?
- Does the structure of the case follow case conventions (e.g., opening hook, closing summary) and have a logical case flow?
- Is the motivation for the case clear based on the case content?
- Is the focal decision well-defined and the situation surrounding it clearly explained?
- Is all of the necessary information contained in the case to answer the suggested discussion questions?
- Will the target students find the case interesting and the discussion engaging?

IM/TN
- Are the case and IM/TN aligned in terms of content?
- Are the learning objectives clear and appropriate for the target students?
- Do the case and IM/TN as currently constructed achieve the learning objectives?
- Is the IM/TN complete with all the required sections for the target outlet in their recommended order?
- Are the suggested discussion questions challenging and the suggested answers and analysis thorough?
- Are the connections to theory and literature appropriate and well documented?
- Is the suggested teaching approach appropriate?

We recommend that in addition to receiving written feedback from your peer reviewer you also try to have a conversation to see what the reviewer's experience was with working through your work. Were there any points where they were confused or frustrated? Did the order of the information as presented in the case make sense? Was the case interesting to them or did they find it predictable? Did they find the case and IM/TN to be consistent and aligned, or were they surprised by the IM/TN contents after reading the case? Were there any topics or information in either document that they felt were missing, or that would add value to the case? Do they have any suggestions for where to submit the case? How close to ready do they think it is? Having this kind of open discussion in addition to feedback on the writing is important and can really help an author assess how close the work is to submission ready. Remember that a peer review at this stage is intended to be *friendly*; reviewers at this stage will probably not be as critical as the formal peer reviewers will be when you submit your work for publication. Therefore, be careful not to assume the case is ready for submission just because you get an enthusiastic initial response. See if you can push for areas of improvement and ensure you give your colleague sufficient time to review your work in detail. Lastly, always return the favour to colleagues who help you out as friendly reviewers.

Academic Conferences

In addition to friendly peer review, another way to get feedback on your cases prior to submission for publication is to share your work at academic conferences. It has been our experience that authors involved in case tracks at conferences or at academic conferences specifically devoted to case writing are generous with their advice on how to improve your case. The case writing community is a very embracing, developmental, global one and we strongly encourage you to take advantage of it as soon as possible. See the Appendix at the end of the book for a list of organizations with case tracks at their conferences.

As we have mentioned, some academic conferences have case tracks for case researchers to showcase their work. There are two different paths through which case researchers can use these conferences to improve their work: case embryo or cases in development tracks for initial case ideas and cases in progress; and full case tracks for complete cases and IM/TNs that have not yet been submitted for publication. We describe both of these streams below.

Embryo or cases in development

Embryo or cases in development tracks are intended for authors to begin developing a case idea that they have not yet fully written. Most tracks for such cases require authors to submit a one- or two-page summary of what they are considering for the subject of a full case which usually includes a draft opening paragraph. Usually, the summary also briefly outlines the expected learning objectives, target course and audience level, main disciplinary focus, and theories the author anticipates using in the IM/TN. The set of summaries from participating authors is then shared amongst participants to facilitate a discussion. Participants give each author feedback about their initial impressions about the case idea, topic, and learning objectives.

The purpose of embryo tracks is to give authors feedback earlier in the process so other case authors can help shape the case before the author has devoted too much time to it. Sometimes, the outcome is that the author decides it is not an idea worth pursuing. Other times, authors are encouraged to develop a full case and IM/TN and submit it to the conference the following year for deeper feedback. Still other times, authors adapt their plan quite substantially based on the feedback they receive and develop a new idea that has a kernel of what they were originally considering. For example, sometimes reviewers really like the case but recommend a more impactful theoretical lens instead of what the author initially selected. Or the reviewers point out that the case would be better positioned through a different discipline than the one the author comes from, in which case the author could seek a co-author in that field. Embryo tracks are helpful for case authors who want to get early feedback from more experienced authors. The caveat is that as a participant in an embryo track, there is an expectation that you reciprocate the feedback to others about their case ideas, and that all participating authors must be open to hearing different perspectives and opinions about their case ideas. We strongly recommend that new case research authors (and even more experienced case researchers) try an embryo case track if they have the opportunity to participate as they are very developmental.

Full cases

The other option for academic conferences is to submit your case to the full case track, which is typically organized by disciplinary area. Case tracks can be embedded in a traditional academic conference (e.g., Administrative Sciences Association of Canada – ASAC – annual conference) or be a stand-alone case conference (e.g., North American Case Research Association – NACRA – conference). Full case tracks expect to receive a complete case and IM/TN submission, which often combine to be 30 pages or more. Be sure to check to see if there is a page limit for the conference and stick to it if you are going to submit to this track. The idea in this track is that authors have fully developed their case and are submitting a complete set of materials for peer review. Sometimes the cases submitted to the full case track were embryo cases in a previous year, while at other times they are new cases that have not yet had any peer review or feedback; the choice is up to the authors which approach they wish to take. One of the benefits of submitting your completed case and IM/TN to a case conference is that you actually receive two rounds of feedback: one as your case is reviewed for acceptance into the conference; and, if accepted, a second round at the conference itself.

For case writers working in other languages, we note that NACRA's annual conference currently has full case tracks in five other languages: Chinese; French; Portuguese; Russian; and Spanish. NACRA's journal, the *Case Research Journal* (CRJ), however, only publishes in English, so authors writing in languages other than English are encouraged to co-author with native English writers if they wish to publish in the CRJ.

The expectation for the full case track is that both components are fully developed, complete, and ready for detailed review with an aim of moving them towards eventual publication. This should involve a good copy edit to both documents; essentially, try to submit a 'publication-ready' version. Since conferences with case tracks often have affiliations with case publications, case track participants may be best able to provide advice to authors about how to get their case ready for submission at that outlet. However, some conferences are neutral on the outlet and many reviewers have experience with several outlets and can provide strong advice for how to get the case ready for submission elsewhere. Let your fellow participants know what you would like to do with your case so they can target their suggestions accordingly; this is particularly helpful in terms of guidance related to the IM/TN. The quid pro quo is that you are expected to read and provide your detailed feedback and suggestions on the other participants' work which is usually distributed in advance for that purpose. If your case is developed enough to submit to a full case track, we highly recommend attending a case conference to develop it further. Keep in mind that updates to your case between the time of submission and the time of the conference are usually welcome so that you can get feedback on your most recent version. Just be sure to share any updates with your track chair well in advance so your fellow attendees can prepare feedback on the newest version.

A point to remember is if you do submit your case to a conference and it is selected to be part of the proceedings, we do not recommend you include the full case as some case publishing outlets consider this as technically published. Many case conferences will give you the option to just include the case abstract in the proceedings, which is a safer option. Whichever path you choose, embryo or full case track (and we strongly recommend both), the experience of working with fellow case researchers can be very motivating and inspiring in addition to being practically helpful for developing your work for publication. Case conferences can be a terrific investment in developing your case research skills and becoming known in the case research community. We have found the global case writing community to be a very welcoming and collaborative group!

TESTING YOUR CASE

One of the final and best ways to know whether your case is ready for publication is to test it out using one of three potential testing forums: classroom cases; case competitions; and assignment or examination cases.

Classrooms

In our opinion, the best way to test a case is to use it for the first time in a classroom and see how it goes! After all the work you have put into the case by this point, it can be an exciting step to get to put your work into the hands of students.

One of the biggest challenges in testing a case in a classroom is finding a course in which to test it. If you are lucky, you will be able to test the case in your own classroom by slotting it into your course syllabus at the next available opportunity. Testing out a new case that their instructor has written can be really fun for students because they know you are invested in the case and they know you know it very well, and are likely to include additional information about the topic that didn't make it into the case itself. Students enjoy learning from cases that their instructors have written as it is fun for them to see that all the cases they use in their programme are written by instructors just like you.

However, if you take that approach, it is useful to have a colleague (maybe a co-author or your friendly case reviewer) attend as well to take notes. If you are busy trying to teach the case, it is really challenging to be comprehensive in terms of noticing all of the engagement in the classroom and being able to take notes in real time while the insight is still fresh in your head. If that's not possible, ask a student or graduate student to observe and take notes for you. Another option is to tape or video record the class so you can review it afterwards. If you are already teaching the class online, recording through a method such as Zoom or Microsoft Teams provides an easy way to capture all of the interaction, demonstrating the sections that engage students and those that need to be augmented or removed. Finally, you can also use the students themselves as a source of feedback. After you teach the case for the first time, give students a chance to express how the case worked for them and whether they have any insights into how to improve it. Students love being able to shape the development of a case. You can use a simple survey for them to fill out, either online or as a paper version distributed at the end of class. We recommend you provide a way for students to give this feedback anonymously as there is a power differential that exists when you are their current instructor and are asking for comments on something you have created. We are willing to bet that you will be surprised at the level of insight your students can have about what makes for effective cases! Be sure students understand that the draft case is not for distribution as you intend to publish it eventually.

Sometimes you will not have an opportunity to test a case in your own classroom or your co-author's class in a reasonable time frame. One option is to ask another instructor to test your case for you instead. In that situation, you can help the other instructor prepare for the class and then either be the in-class observer or a guest instructor for that session. In the sense that your objective as the author is to enable other instructors to effectively teach the class using your materials, being the observer is a very realistic way to test your case. Peers teaching your case will not have your in-depth understanding of the material and the limitations of the case will be more readily observable. They may decide to highlight different elements, or the timing may end up being shorter or longer than anticipated. If you happen to have the opportunity to use both methods (you teach the case with another instructor observing and another instructor teaches your case with you observing), you could do one first followed by the second after the revisions from the first test are complete. This thorough approach would be a double check that the revisions are in fact an improvement to the case that resolve any prior issues. The bottom line is that however you test your case, the feedback you get about what works and what does not is invaluable for the further development of your work, both on this case and on future cases. For that reason, many outlets strongly suggest that cases be test taught before they are published.

Here are key factors to consider when testing the case in class:

• How did the students respond to the case in terms of engagement level?

- Were there any aspects of the case that they did not understand? What did you say to help clarify these elements and how can you incorporate that into case revisions?
- Were the assignment questions effective in prompting discussion?
- Was there enough information to sustain the class for the full time frame?
- Was the case balanced enough that there were diverse opinions supported by case data?
- Did the case meet the identified learning objectives?
- Do you think that an instructor could teach the case effectively using only the materials you have provided in your case and IM/TN?

Any approach that you take in class to address concerns about any of the above factors should be incorporated into your revisions. Finally, be sure to explain in your IM/TN how the case was tested and what revisions were made in response. Sometimes authors expand on this information in the letter to the editor when they submit the case to their target outlet.

Case Competitions

Another approach to testing a case is to try it out in a case competition instead of a classroom. Broadly, there are two types of case competitions: a general call for cases on a particular topic where the winning case receives a prize and is often eligible for publication; and a call for cases which are then used as part of a student case analysis competition. In the latter example, case competitions regularly need new cases that are unpublished and do not have online solutions available to competing teams so the competition can be fair. While the format for how a case competition case is used is of course different from how we use cases in class, a case competition can nevertheless be helpful to an author. For example, the work students do in a case competition can clearly show the author whether the issues intended to be raised in the case came through in the case analysis. Also, the competition can show the extent to which students were clear about the issues and focal decision in the case. Lastly, competitions can raise perspectives, issues, and solutions that the author may not have thought of but that the students correctly identify. Overall, case competitions provide a limited set of feedback on a case relative to an in-class test, but authors can still get a lot of value from testing a case this way. Case competitions are held around the world with many of them occurring annually, and are typically sponsored by academic institutions, organizations, and case publishers. Be sure to mark the case as draft and not for distribution if you agree to let a competition use your case. See the Appendix at the end of the book for a listing of case competitions around the world.

Assignments/Examinations

One final method for testing a case is to use it either as a student assignment case (group or individual) or as an examination case (Andrews, 2021). Again, this method provides only indirect feedback on the IM/TN compared to an in-class delivery of the case, but it can nevertheless provide some data about whether students understand the case issues properly, whether there is enough data in the case to answer the examination questions, and whether the analysis instructors should expect from strong students is accurate. Sometimes, student insight in response to exam questions on the case includes new ideas and innovative analysis that can be incorporated into the case, or be included in an exhibit in an IM/TN. Just like case competitions, instructors are regularly in need of new cases without available online solutions in order to set fair assignments and exams. For more on the use of cases for examinations, see Wood et al. (2018).

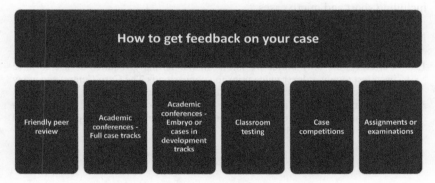

Figure 9.1   *Ways to get feedback on your case*

KEY CHAPTER TAKEAWAYS

- Our strong advice is to set yourself up for success and test your case as soon as possible, ideally before you submit to a peer-reviewed outlet. The benefits of feedback from a friendly review or a conference workshop process are many and we think they are very much worth your time investment.
- Increasingly, it is becoming an expectation of editors and reviewers to test your case prior to publication.
- When you are ready, consider testing your case in your own classroom with a colleague observing, or swapping roles and testing it in your colleague's classroom instead.

- If you cannot find a course in which to test your case, consider submitting it for use by a case competition, or using it as a student assignment, or as an examination case.
- Getting into the habit of gathering as much feedback from a range of sources prior to submission to a publication outlet will greatly improve the odds of your work being well received during the review process at your target outlet. Chances are you will receive reviewer feedback that you have heard before and can respond to effectively.
- Being able to provide an account of how a case was received by a class and how you already addressed any issues increases your credibility with reviewers and editors alike.
- Learn to lean into all kinds of feedback on your cases but of course the final version of your case and IM/TN is up to you.

In Chapter 10 we will review different forms of cases besides the traditional narrative format as there are interesting new formats emerging in the field, including short and micro cases.

NOTES

1. Currently, the only outlet we know of that formally requires a case to have been test taught at least twice prior to submission is The Case Centre; see www .thecasecentre.org/submission/guidelines/requirements.
2. For example, see Emerald Publishing's *The CASE Journal* at https://caseshub.em eraldgrouppublishing.com/courses/have-you-covered-everything/#/page/5c2d d944c7bd2e32fd18b08f.

10. Special types of cases

VENTURING BEYOND TRADITIONAL CASE FORMATS

The previous chapters have led you through the typical processes for deciding what kind of case to write, determining the type of data you are going to be using (primary or secondary), creating a case framework to guide the case development, and finally, how to actually start writing the case and instructor's manual or teaching note (IM/TN). We have presented this information for the 'standard' case format which normally is eight to 10 pages of narrative text with four to five additional pages of exhibits for the case itself (up to 15 pages total), accompanied by a robust IM/TN. However, as noted in Chapter 1, case journals and publishers are expanding the boundaries of the formats they will accept for cases with a goal of providing stronger engagement and connection with students while maintaining the core elements of what makes cases effective teaching tools. This chapter presents alternative formats for cases that can be used in your classroom, for examination purposes, in textbooks, or for special calls from case journals and publishers. These include short (and micro) cases, video cases, multi-media cases, graphic cases, flipped classroom cases, live cases, student-written, instructor-facilitated (SWIF) cases, and podcast or audio cases.

Short and Micro Cases

The most prevalent of new case formats include short and micro cases. Short cases are exactly what they sound like: cases that are significantly shorter than the average case length. Short cases are usually up to six pages including both text and exhibits, although each outlet has a different page or word limit for what they consider a short case. Short cases are intended to be able to be read in under 15 minutes. Micro cases are even more compact, one to two pages of text and exhibits that can be read in under five minutes. Both types of cases can be based on either primary or secondary sources. Short and micro cases provide the flexibility to instructors of introducing a case into a class environment in real time, followed by the discussion and analysis. Students like them because they are not required to read 15 pages of case narrative and exhibits.

Instructors like assigning short cases because they know more students will have read them, or that only a brief period of class time needs to be dedicated for students to get prepared. This format takes the guesswork out of whether or not students will be prepared, and how to manage it if they are not.

The downside for instructors is that short and micro cases, by their nature, have less content and so instructors need to plan ahead for how the case discussion will unfold. Writing short and micro cases requires real skill as authors must find a way to fit in all of the necessary information for a robust case analysis into a shorter framework. This requires the case to have a tight focus, exploring a smaller number of topics (perhaps only one) than in a longer case. The case outline is even more important for short and micro cases given that every section, sentence and word should only be included if it is critical to the case analysis. The writing needs to be crisp and to the point, engaging the reader immediately.

While new case writers often believe that short cases are a good place to start, we believe that writing short and micro cases is a big challenge for authors. In addition to the writing issues, short cases also present a challenge in terms of topic choice as some lend themselves to the kind of extreme focus this type of case requires, while other topics do not. In our experience, this judgement call is better made by experienced case authors. That said, authors can always try to write their case as a short one, and if it proves too complex for that format, move to develop the case into a regular length one instead. For the same reasons, we also believe that micro cases can be the most difficult type to write.

While short cases are briefer, the IM/TNs accompanying short and micro cases are just as robust and detailed as they are for traditional cases. As such, authors of short and micro cases may find that their IM/TN is easily many times the length of the case itself. We stress this point because the brevity of short and micro cases requires even more direction on how the case should evolve in the classroom and how it should be tied to core theories and frameworks.

Increasingly, there are more calls and competitions from case journals and publishers for short and micro cases (e.g., *The Case Research Journal*, The Case Centre, and *The CASE Journal*), demonstrating the growing interest from educators and students for shorter cases. Remember though, short and micro cases can be tricky to take through a review process as case reviewers often keep asking authors to add in additional information while maintaining the required case length. Short and micro cases are nevertheless usually designed to be used in classrooms for regular class periods such as 60 to 90 minutes. This means that even short cases about focused topics often have multiple learning objectives that have to be met. Consequently, all of the usual sections in an IM/TN are required to be as comprehensive as in any other longer case.

Hence, the work involved in developing an IM/TN for a short or micro case is essentially equivalent to that for a longer case.

Video Cases

There is a range of ways in which a video format can be incorporated into a case. Most video cases involve interviews or supporting material that have been videotaped to use in the classroom to support the written case narrative. Frequently, the supporting video is not required for the case to be used effectively but rather a nice-to-have support for the class session to be more engaging and increase the richness of the case data. In other words, students who do not access the video can still achieve the case learning objectives even if it is not as fun as for those who do. In other scenarios, the video component of the case is crucial to the design of the case and without it the case learning objectives cannot be properly met (e.g., Sharen, 2016). Whether the video content is vital or not, often the written case is shorter because it is supplemented in the classroom by the use of the video information. Note that video components also vary according to whether they are designed to be used with the full set of students in class, or whether they are designed to be viewed prior to class. Lastly, the number of videos can differ, with some cases having only one video component while others have several from which instructors can choose. Sometimes these video resources include a 'what happened' epilogue video that instructors can show to students at the conclusion of the case discussion.

Years ago, video cases meant ordering the video material which was available through the case publisher on VHS tapes. These were eventually replaced by DVDs, and now authors submitting video cases can upload their videos to case publishers who provide them, along with the case as downloadable files, often MP4s, although the specific format will depend on the individual publisher. One of the challenges about video cases is figuring out how the video can be stored and accessed long term if the publisher cannot provide a permanent online location. Some publishers use public video platforms such as Vimeo for this purpose.

The majority of video cases include recorded interviews with individuals noted in the case, usually the case protagonist. These interviews can be done in a one-on-one setting with the representative from the focal company, or we have seen video cases where the representative has been invited to a class while the case is being taught and recorded when they comment during various sections of the case discussion. Video cases are more challenging to create than traditional cases as they require someone to record and edit the interviews. Once the videos have been completed, the individual(s) interviewed (and the company) are also required to sign off on the videos in terms of content as well as explicit permission to distribute the video file along with the case. It is always a clever idea, prior to spending a lot of time creating a video case, to determine whether your publication target accepts them as you may either need to revert back to a traditional case or change your selected publication outlet.

Despite these challenges, video cases are worth pursuing because students really enjoy the opportunity to see the focal individuals in your case. Adding video can also make the case more dynamic as video information is presented at key points in the case analysis to move the case narrative along. Lastly, effective supplementary videos can make your case more popular, so it is worth exploring this option if you have a protagonist (and ideally others at your focal company) who is open to creating a video. For all these reasons, we anticipate that the market for video cases will continue to grow.

Multi-Media Cases

Multi-media cases can be seen as an expansion of video cases in that they often include video clips that have been recorded in first person interviews, but they also have dynamic links to other web-based materials and have other case-related content. From an instructor perspective, multi-media cases offer high student engagement and potential learning, albeit often at a high per-student cost especially if you face additional expense due to foreign exchange rates. Despite the costs, instructors often include one or two such cases in their syllabus because they are among the students' favourite cases.

From an author perspective, multi-media cases are much more complex to design, create, and produce given the expertise required to obtain the interviews and receive permission to use the online content. While incredibly engaging for students, we recommend that multi-media cases be left to experienced case writers that are working in a professional team that has special expertise related to video production and editing. We distinguish between video cases and multi-media cases because while a number of case journals and publishers have the ability to incorporate downloadable files including videos, PowerPoint presentations, Excel spreadsheets, and presentation slides for broader distribution, only a small number are able to host truly multi-media cases (e.g., Harvard Business Publishing). If you are interested in creating a multi-media case, we strongly encourage you to reach out to your target case publication to make sure you are aware of their technology formats and requirements prior to getting started. Ensure you have a strong pedagogical rationale for why your case idea will enhance learning more as a multi-media than in another format. If you are able to host your multi-media case on your own website (or your institution's website), some case publishers like The Case Centre (2022) will partner with you to help you distribute and publicize it.[1] If you want to get a better sense of the format of multi-media cases, the Harvard Business Publishing website has some great examples across a number of academic disciplines. Some of our favourites include 'Eataly: reimagining the grocery store' (Gupta et al., 2015) and 'Leadership, culture, and transition at lululemon' (Tushman et al., 2010).

Graphic Cases

Graphic cases are a new innovation in case writing. They present a significant divergence from the traditional case format of narrative text supported by exhibits in that they have much more in common with graphic novels or manga formats. The information to be conveyed is done through pictures with dialogue and description of the action in the case. The creation process for a graphic case requires a few more steps. It begins with the same core elements as a traditional case: identifying a topic; researching the case; and writing the case. However, this then needs to be translated into creating a script to guide the development of a storyboard which is transformed into the final graphic version of the case. It also requires the case writer (unless they are also extremely talented) to source an artist to help with the migration of the case from purely written text to images that tell a compelling story while remaining true to the case purpose. Similar to traditional cases, graphic cases are normally accompanied by a fully developed IM/TN in a standard format.

Graphic cases are still quite rare in classrooms, although recent special calls for case journals have included the opportunity for the submission of graphic cases alongside other alternative case formats such as short and micro cases, video cases, and multi-media cases. If you are considering authoring a graphic format case, we recommend you consider why the graphic format is preferable to other formats from a pedagogical perspective. For instance, will students be able to achieve certain learning objectives by using a graphic case that they would not be able to in another format? While graphic cases are becoming more common, we expect that publishers, editors, and reviewers will prefer graphic cases that have a clear rationale for using that format rather than merely viewing the format as a gimmick. Examples of graphic cases can be found through The Case Centre, who offer a library of over 30 cases available in graphic and cartoon format.[2]

Flipped Classroom Cases

Traditional case writing is based on the idea that all of the information for the analysis of the case is contained in the case narrative and exhibits. Students prepare the case prior to the start of the class and come in, ready to discuss the case in a class discussion led and directed by the course instructor. Flipped classrooms build on the increasingly popular blended student-centric model where students take time in the classroom to construct and co-create their learning. Traditional lectures and course information are made available outside of class time through modes including recorded lectures and posted slides (Kaw and Hess, 2007). When students come to class, the time is used in a more applied manner to ensure comprehension.

A flipped classroom case is a variation of this model. Cases are much more stripped down, containing the core information necessary to set the students in the right direction. Students are encouraged to go beyond the case information and do their own research about what they believe to be crucial elements of the case. This work can be done in the classroom or an online setting, with students working individually or in teams to identify and think through the case issues. Flipped classroom cases can be interesting for case authors as they provide more flexibility in working on case topics that may still be evolving (more of that below with live cases). Flipped classroom cases still include a robust IM/TN which incorporates more variation into its analysis given the cases are not as structured as traditional cases. As traditional classrooms begin to incorporate flipped classroom models more often, there will eventually be a stronger demand for flipped classroom cases. To our knowledge, there are very few (if any) case journals and publishers who accept flipped classroom cases for publication; the most common application is for purpose written cases for in-class use by individual instructors.

Live Cases

Live cases differ from traditional cases in several ways, the first being that the focal issue has not been resolved at the time of the case writing (Andrews, 2021). Second, the case process incorporates real-time interaction between students and the case organization (Woodwark and Schnarr, 2022). In a live case, the focal company participates in the process in real time as students help problem-solve a current issue, grounded in a written case and supporting materials, that the organization is facing (Naumes and Naumes, 2015; Rapp and Ogilvie, 2019). Markulis outlined three additional features required for a live case: '1. personal participation and appearance by the company's decision-makers during the case presentation and discussion, 2. the immediate accessibility of the company for the students, 3. the company situation or strategic decision is one that has just been made or is about to be made' (1985, p. 169). Although we agree with these points, in our opinion it is also important to point out that live cases are designed for students to conduct analysis using data outside the case to propose solutions. This is a key difference from traditional case analysis where students are expected to limit themselves to the case data provided.

While there is a lot of blurring in the academic research related to defining live cases (e.g., they are sometimes conflated with consulting projects with no written case element), live cases are engaging as they are opportunities for a connection between the focal company and students on issues unfolding in real time. The opportunity for having a real impact on the case organization – or even to be hired by the firm – is extremely motivating for students. The elements in and format of a live case are similar to a traditional case, and the case writing process mirrors what was outlined in previous chapters. The only real difference is that case authors do not have the luxury of knowing 'what happened' when writing the case document. Live cases are fantastic for use in case competitions and in classes, particularly if representatives from the focal company can be there in person or virtually to listen to the student analysis and proposed solutions. We have had the opportunity to write many live cases with local, national, and multinational organizations, some of which have evolved into published cases (Schnarr and Kunsch, 2016; Woodwark et al., 2020b). Most live cases can be developed into publishable cases after the live component is over by reverse engineering the learning objectives from the exercise into a full IM/TN. While they are not as prevalent, there are case publishers (e.g., The Case Centre) who accept live cases.

Student-Written, Instructor-Facilitated (SWIF) Cases

This last category of case is different from the others described in this chapter not because of its format, but rather in how it gets written. SWIF cases involve a student (or group of students) leading the case writing activities, assisted by an academic instructor. We have experience using them as in-class, group exercises, individual research projects, and cases developed for internal and external case competitions or conferences. Again, they can be created as primary or secondary data cases, although if you are doing this as an in-class, group exercise we strongly recommend using a secondary data case approach. In SWIF cases, the product is a case with a truncated IM/TN; students need to be given a template with the relevant case sections (tailored to your academic discipline) and a guide for how to work through the case process step by step. For each section, you will need to provide feedback to help shape the case direction and narrative. While the final case product will look remarkably similar to a published case, students usually do not have the theory expertise of their instructors (exceptions would be doctoral students), and so the IM/TN is a shell of what would be expected in a traditional IM/TN. For SWIF cases, the IM/TN focuses on crafting and answering the discussion questions for the case. This is done during the case writing so students can see the importance of including all of the required information in the case to be able to answer the case questions.

After many years of using cases, students are often excited by the idea of being able to write one. As instructors, we believe SWIF cases are an extremely valuable pedagogical exercise because they tap into a broad range of the essential learning outcomes identified by bodies like the American Association of Colleges & Universities (AAC&U, 2022). A complex project such as writing a new case that relates to pedagogical outcomes is a terrific way to introduce graduate students to the notion of learning objectives, which many will need in their future careers. For a detailed review of the many benefits of case writing for MBA students in particular, see Fairfax and Gong (2022).

If you have not written a case yourself, we would recommend waiting until you have successfully completed a few prior to embarking on a SWIF case as it is a time-consuming process that requires a firm grasp of case writing to create effective student cases. If you are interested in this approach, we have written a guide (along with two colleagues) to assist instructors with this process (Beal et al., 2016). While they can involve a lot of work, SWIF cases are extremely rewarding for both the instructor and the student(s). Unlike case analysis or independent research reports, SWIF cases have an opportunity to be used outside of the classroom, and for the best SWIF cases there is a chance for publication (Ross et al., 2021; Schnarr et al., 2016). Just a note of caution that if you do decide to undertake a SWIF case, temper the expectations for the use of the case beyond the academic exercise; it takes a lot of work to take a SWIF case to one that is at a level that would be considered for publication by a journal or case publisher. Some other ways to highlight SWIF cases could include inviting the authors of the highest graded SWIF case to come back and teach their case the subsequent year or creating a best in show casebook of the top case from each class of your course which gets added to year on year.

Podcast or Audio Cases

As we discussed in Chapter 6 about secondary source cases, a new potential source for case data is podcasts. Podcasts have proliferated over the past decade and are now hugely popular, with most being widely available for free. In our opinion, there is an opportunity for case writers to use podcasts as data sources for written cases, but also for podcasts to be used almost like audio cases. We think the audio-only format of podcasts has a lot of potential for student engagement with the case method. However, this idea is still new enough that most publishing outlets have not yet figured out if or how they are willing to engage with case authors in a podcast or audio format. We expect that in the next few years case publishing outlets are going to have to articulate their policies both about using podcasts as data sources for written cases and authors producing cases in audio-only format for distribution to students instead of in written format. Early audio cases will probably essentially be narrated written cases in simple audio file formats similar to a podcast, but there is clearly an opportunity for case publishers to produce more sophisticated audio cases with multiple voices and sound effects if they choose to develop this kind of case format. We will be watching this potential new space with interest to see how the case market responds. Of interest is that Harvard Business Publishing has recently begun producing *Podcases*, available at https://hbsp .harvard.edu/podcases/.

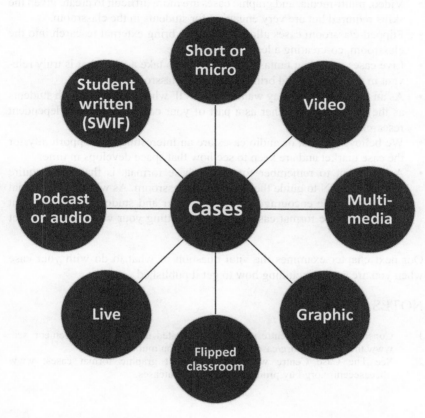

Figure 10.1   Special types of cases

KEY CHAPTER TAKEAWAYS

• While the majority of this book is focused on helping you write a regular case and IM/TN, there are other formats of cases that are being seen more regularly in classrooms and are being accepted by case journals and publishers. These include short (and micro) cases, video cases, multi-media cases, graphic cases, flipped classroom cases, live cases, SWIF cases, and potentially podcast or audio cases in the future.

- Out of all of these additional formats, short cases are the most popular and there are a greater number of opportunities to publish these with case journals and publishers, often through special calls.
- Video, multi-media, and graphic cases are more difficult to create given the skills required but are very engaging for students in the classroom.
- Flipped-classroom cases allow students to bring external research into the classroom, co-creating a learning experience.
- Live cases provide a fantastic opportunity to take a topic that is truly relevant in the moment and bring it into your classroom.
- As an instructor, you may want to try SWIF where you work with students as they write a case either as a part of your course or as an independent research exercise.
- We believe podcast or audio cases are an interesting new opportunity for the case market and are keen to see how that space develops in time.
- A key point to remember for all of these formats is that they require a robust IM/TN to guide their use in the classroom. As with the traditional case format, we encourage you to seek peer and student feedback about your alternative format case prior to submitting your work to your target outlet.

Our next chapter examines the vital question of what to do with your case when you are ready, including how to get it published.

NOTES

1.   Consider The Case Centre if you are interested in such an arrangement; see: www.thecasecentre.org/caseWriting/distribution/multimedia.
2.   See The Case Centre website page about graphic format cases: www .thecasecentre.org/buy/products/graphicformatcases.

11. How to get your case published

For many of us, the ultimate goal of writing a case is getting it published, either by an academic journal (e.g., *Case Research Journal*, *The CASE Journal*), a case distribution house (e.g., Ivey Publishing, The Case Centre), or in a textbook related to your discipline. While publishing your case will allow it to be experienced by the maximum number of students, there are other ways to use your case beyond these avenues, including using your case in the classroom, as exams, in textbooks, and case competitions. This chapter will discuss what you can do with a finished, polished case, how to work through the publication process, and how to make your case more visible once it has been published.

We note that while we have focused on publication options in English, cases are published in plenty of other languages too. In fact, some publishers and distribution houses publish translations of cases originally published in English given sufficient demand (e.g., Ivey Publishing offers some cases in simplified Chinese).

WHAT CAN YOU DO WITH A FINISHED, POLISHED CASE?

The previous chapters have walked you through how to write a case and instructor's manual or teaching note (IM/TN) and how to test your case. Once those steps are completed, you have a number of options for how to use your case. While there are many advantages to having your case formally published, including credit at your academic institution, making some money through royalties, and having your case used by classrooms around the world, there are also some disadvantages. The publication process can take a long time and the review process (particularly for academic journals) can be challenging when reviewers want you to change your case in a way that does not fit with your case vision. Ideally, before you get started writing your case you have already thought through what you would like to do with it when it is done as that will dictate some of your choices for the case and IM/TN structure as well as content. Later on in this chapter we will discuss the publication process in more detail, but we will start out with the suite of options for a finished case.

OPPORTUNITIES FOR USE

This section is organized into two categories: non-publication uses for cases; and publication vehicles for cases. The first group includes simply using your cases in your classes (or those of your peers), for evaluation purposes, or for internal student case competitions; we have also discussed some of these uses in Chapter 9, which looked at testing your case. The second group includes publishing your case in peer-reviewed academic journals, through case publishing/distribution houses, in case writing competitions, or in textbooks.

Non-published: Classroom Use

In Chapter 9 we wrote about the importance of testing your case in a classroom prior to submitting it for publication. However, many case authors write cases with the intention of never having them published, but rather solely for use in their classrooms. There are a few reasons why this occurs. Sometimes instructors want to focus on a narrow issue in their course to highlight a specific theory or framework that is perhaps less widely used, and the best way to do that is to write a custom case about it since few, if any, appropriate options exist. These are targeted cases that are specifically written to give students experience with the selected issue. While this sounds a lot like the motivation for a regular case, often the topic is specific enough that it would not have broader appeal in the market. For instance, sometimes instructors just cannot find a case on their topic focused in their geographic area. Also, some classes have students who are highly specialized, and previously published cases do not adequately meet their learning needs. Finally, sometimes instructors enjoy writing their own cases and have no interest in the publication process.

Cases targeted only for classroom use have more flexibility in terms of case length, format, and exhibits because the only reviewer is the author themself. While most published cases have the goal of being used during a single class (often 80 minutes), purpose written cases can be for any length of time. They can also be fictional cases, not based on an actual event but written to illustrate a specific teaching point. Fictional cases are very difficult to get published so if you are interested in writing a fictional case, this is a possible use for it (along with evaluation purposes outlined below). Of course, the case should still present all of the relevant information, be interesting, have a good case hook, and be well-written. If you create a classroom use case based on primary data, we still recommend getting sign-off from the company just to protect yourself and your institution in case something changes in the future.

The goal of classroom use cases is to make the case as relevant and workable for the class context the author is intending to use it for. It is also a much faster process to complete than cases intended for a publication channel because once the case is written it can be used immediately. Cases intended only for classroom use can be less formal than those intended for publication. There is no requirement for a formal IM/TN to be created, although it is a good idea if the author has an idea of the learning objectives for the case and how it is going to roll out in the classroom when it is taught. However, if there is a chance the case will be used by a colleague or by your teaching team if it is part of a coordinated course, authors may want to create an informal IM/TN with discussion questions and answers, teaching plan and board plan. This gives your peers some guidance in terms of how the case should unfold in the classroom.

Non-published: Evaluation Purposes

One of the challenges of case-based evaluations is that there are often case solutions available on the internet for cases that have already been published, particularly if they have been around for a few years. A way to address this is to create an original case with the purpose of using it for a case analysis assignment, a midterm, or a final exam. Similar to classroom use cases, authors have flexibility to custom create a case in terms of length and the case can be decision-based or descriptive and be factual, disguised, or fictional. Again, there is no need for a formal IM/TN for evaluation cases, but it is good to create thorough answers to the assignment questions, which often involves completing the required analysis being asked of students.

As outlined in Chapter 9, evaluation cases can start out as an internally crafted case for a midterm, case analysis assignment, or a final exam, and then can be used in the classroom or even be sent externally to be published as long as there is also a well-developed IM/TN. It is worth noting that classroom use cases and evaluation cases could also be the result of cases that were originally intended for publication but were not successful. While we hope that all of your submitted cases get published, it is good to know that if that does not happen, there are still worthy uses for your case.

Non-published: Internal Student Case Competitions

Some institutions hold internal or external student case competitions which provide an opportunity to create custom cases. Given the focal company and the topic being explored, it is sometimes not possible to publish the case after the competition. We have been involved in writing many cases for internal case competitions and only a fraction have had the opportunity for publication after the competition has been completed. Case competitions are a great chance to practise your case writing skills. They are often primary data cases, so it is also an opportunity to hone your ability to work with the focal company through the initial discovery, interview, and writing process. As the final intent for the case is pre-determined – the case competition – there is no pressure from the company to see their case in print. Similar to classroom use and evaluation cases, there is no formal requirement to create a robust IM/TN although as a courtesy to the case competition judges, they should be provided with proposed solutions to the questions being asked of the students. If you do have the ability to publish the case after the case competition ends, our strong recommendation is to determine the publication outlet, craft the IM/TN, and get it submitted to a case journal or case distribution house as soon as possible. There is nothing as frustrating as letting the case linger for a while and then discovering your case contacts are no longer at the organization, meaning that it is far more difficult to obtain the required release to publish.

It is also worth noting that there are a limited number of international student case competitions that do accept cases from outside their own institution (e.g., the cases are not all crafted by the host institution of the case competition). This is another possible use for your case but if you do so just be careful to check that you retain ownership of your case and that the use of the case in that type of competition does not result in it being considered previously published by academic journals or case distribution houses. One way to address any concern about prior usage is to frame the case competition use as a way of testing the case in a non-classroom format.

Published: Academic Journals

There are a number of peer-reviewed academic journals that accept teaching cases. These include journals that are purely case based, some that also accept articles related to case-based education, and a small subset of journals that also accept cases along with 'traditional' research articles. Some of the journals accept cases across all business disciplines, while others are focused in a specific area (e.g., information technology). The majority of these journals have a double-blind, peer-review process and require a detailed IM/TN in order for the case to be considered. Additional details about the publishing process in such outlets are provided below in this chapter. If you are interested in publishing your case in an academic journal, it is important to target an outlet before you even start writing the case and IM/TN as case journals have a wide variation about requirements in terms of the case length, format, focus, and what must be included in the IM/TN. Some case journals only accept decision-based, factual cases based on primary data sources. Others will accept descriptive cases, or cases using composite or even fictional data. Each journal has its own set of author instructions that details what kinds of cases are and are not acceptable for submission (e.g., Emerald Publishing Group, 2022; Ivey Publishing, n.d.).

The cases published in major academic journals (such as the *Case Research Journal*) are also available through case distributors (e.g., Harvard Business Publishing, Ivey Publishing). If the publisher provides royalties for when your case is used by external sources, the homepage for the journal will also provide details as to the percentage that comes back to the case author. The journal homepage will often include information about the targeted review time after the case is submitted and the impact factor of the journal. The impact factor of the journal may be important if you intend to use the published case as part of your promotion package.

There are a number of case journals that are associated with case writing and research associations. For example, the North American Case Research Association (NACRA) publishes the *Case Research Journal*, while the Society for Case Research publishes three journals: the *Business Case Journal*; the *Journal of Critical Incidents*; and the *Journal of Case Studies*. Many of these associations hold annual meetings where there is an opportunity to meet the editors of these journal(s) and get first-hand information about what they are looking for in relation to case submissions. Case journals also sometimes do special issues on interesting topics, which could provide an opportunity to explore your case writing abilities. Examples of special issue calls from case journals have included alternative format cases (e.g., video, graphic), short/ micro cases, cases related to specific geographics or industries, and cases on underrepresented protagonists. The Appendix to this book provides a select list of peer-reviewed academic journals that accept cases.

Case Publishing and Distribution Houses

Case publishing and distribution houses are slightly different concepts, but we group them here together as they are often considered in tandem. Case publishers are organizations that both accept and sometimes distribute cases. There are a number of academic institutions that only accept and publish cases authored by faculty from their own institution (e.g., Darden Business Publishing at the University of Virginia, HEC Montréal Case Centre). Other organizations both accept and publish cases for distribution from external sources. Often, these case publishers also have partnerships to distribute cases from academic journals or other case publishers, giving them a broader audience. Both Ivey Publishing and the Case Centre publish and distribute original cases as well as distribute cases from partner organizations. It is important to note that one of the most well-known case houses, Harvard Business Publishing, only accepts original cases from Harvard Business School faculty, but it does distribute cases from a number of academic journals, associations, and partner case publishers. It sounds confusing, but the main takeaway is that there are a number of different avenues for you to publish your case outside of academic journals.

Case publishers can have a shorter publication process than case journals, and the review process, while thorough, can be less onerous. If you are fortunate to be at an institution that publishes its own cases, but has a distribution partnership with a case distributor, you may find that it is the fastest way to get your case officially published, depending on your school's internal case review process. While case publishers do not have an impact factor, they will often provide information about case sales, including the volume of your sales and where they were sold geographically, which can be used to support the educational impact of your cases when going up for promotion (if relevant).

Similar to the advice provided in the previous section on publishing in academic journals, it is important to have a strong understanding of the submission requirements for case publishing houses. There are often significant differences in terms of the case length, formatting requirements, and the required sections in the IM/TN. The Appendix to this book provides a reference list of case publishing and distribution houses that accept and distribute cases.

Case Writing Competitions

A lesser-known opportunity for case publication can come through case writing competitions. There are a number of international case writing competitions that provide an opportunity to submit an unpublished case on a specific topic in exchange for the chance to win a cash prize and be officially published. These are sponsored by large academic publishers, public policy organizations, academic institutions, case journals, and case publishers. They often have restrictions in terms of who can submit (e.g., authors from a specific geographical area, students) and the case topic for the competition. The Appendix to this book provides a reference list of organizations that regularly offer case writing competitions.

Textbooks

Across a number of academic disciplines, there are textbooks that will publish cases to support the theory that is explained. Cases can be positioned in various places in the text: at the beginning of the chapter to frame the content; embedded within the chapter (often as a mini case) to illustrate a particular point; at the end of the chapter to allow the student to apply what they just learned; or as a group of cases at the end of the textbook once all of the theory has been presented. It is less likely that, particularly early in your case writing career, you will publish your cases in textbooks.

Cases generally are sourced for textbooks in a few different ways. They can be created by the author (or author team) of the textbook in order to ensure synergy between the theory and application in the book. Cases in textbooks can be sourced from cases that have already been published by other case publishers. In that situation, case authors sometimes do not even know that their case has been used in a textbook as it is arranged by the case publisher; they will receive a small stipend for their case being used but do not receive a royalty for their case in each textbook that is sold. Established case authors can be approached to write cases for upcoming textbooks where the textbook author does not have that capability. Finally, case authors can reach out to publishers of well-known textbooks that contain cases and offer to provide a case for a future edition. While having your case included in a textbook will potentially expand its reach, early in your case writing career we recommend first focusing on publication in an academic journal or through a case publishing organization.

Figure 11.1   How can my case be used?

WHAT YOU NEED TO KNOW BEFORE YOU SUBMIT A CASE FOR PUBLICATION

Throughout this book, we have tried to highlight how you can set yourself up for success in case writing from first principles. This is particularly true if your ultimate goal is to have your case published. Before you even start writing a case, determine your case publication outlet. We recommend talking to established case writers about your idea and getting their advice about publication targets as well as how to manage the publication process at that particular outlet. Your choice of publication outlet could be dependent on internal factors. Maybe your academic institution will only count it towards tenure if it is published through a peer-reviewed academic journal, or your business school has a case publishing arm, and you are required to publish through them. Perhaps your topic is extremely relevant at the moment and so you would like to get it published as soon as possible. You may be presenting a draft at an academic conference which has a journal attached that publishes cases and you feel it will receive a warmer reception as a result. Your choice of publication outlet may also depend on whether the journal is open access, which will require a fee from you (or your institution on your behalf) if it is accepted for publication.

Once you have (tentatively) decided on a publication outlet, reach out to the case publisher and ask them if there are gaps in their current case catalogue or areas they are looking to highlight. Ask if they already have a case in their publication pipeline on your focal company that is likely to be published in the short term. We have done both of these things, and it both unlocked potential case topics and saved us a lot of future heartbreak when one of our early case ideas turned out to be in the queue for publication at our target outlet. While we could have still written the case and submitted it somewhere else, remember that it would have minimized the impact of the case in the broader academic environment if there were two similar cases in the market at the same time.

Follow the Instructions

The most critical piece of advice we can provide to new case writers is to follow the instructions from your target outlet in terms of case length, format, references, exhibits, and sourcing. Determine the tense in which they require the case to be written including for quotations. Understand whether the case has to be factual, or whether they accept disguised, composite, or fictional cases. Find out whether it has to be a decision-based case or if they also accept descriptive cases. Does the case have to use primary data, or can it be a case written purely on secondary data sources? How do they define secondary data, as this varies between publishers? What sections and content do they require in their IM/TNs? Does the publishing outlet only accept cases from faculty or PhD students or from instructors in a specific country? Again, uncovering this information upfront will make sure that you increase your chance of success at your publication target. Many case publishers will just desk reject a case that does not meet the stated case guidelines. Case publishers will tell you exactly what they are looking for from a submission perspective; do yourself a favour and listen to them! Finally, make sure you give you case a good copy proof-read before it is formally submitted to eliminate errors in spelling, grammar, language, tense, punctuation, and formatting.

WORKING THROUGH THE PUBLICATION PROCESS

Steps in the Publication Process

The steps for having your case published in an academic journal that accepts cases are really no different from the process followed for standard academic journal articles. This begins with your case and IM/TN being uploaded through the submission process of the target journal. They will also ask for all of the standard submission information including authors, institutions, contact information, and often keywords and the case abstract. Once formally submitted to the journal, you will receive a confirmation it has been received. Then the waiting begins. Sometimes when cases are not submitted with complete information (e.g., incomplete IM/TN), did not meet the scope of the journal, or did not follow the submission guidelines, your case will be desk rejected without receiving any reviews. While this is not the outcome you want to have, use it as an opportunity to reflect on what you could do to strengthen your case and IM/TN for future steps.

If your case is not desk rejected, it will go out for review usually in a double-blind, peer-review process to at least two reviewers (sometimes three). The reviewers go through the case and IM/TN and provide feedback, making a recommendation to the editor whether to accept the case (with minor or major revisions) or to reject it. The editor decides whether the case will proceed and works with the author and the reviewers to further iterate the case either until it is acceptable to the majority of reviewers and the editor, or until the author determines that they will not be able to meet the requests of the reviewers and withdraws the case, potentially to submit to a different case journal. If accepted, the case goes through a final edit and then is slated for publication in a future issue of the journal. Depending on the journal, the timeline between initial submission and publication can be anywhere from one to three years in our experience.

Case publishing houses use a similar process, although we have found the review process to be as thorough but more informal. At Ivey Publishing for example, the case is blind reviewed by one or more full-time Ivey Faculty with expertise in the topic area. Through this process, the faculty reviewers may ask for revisions to the case and teaching note or for the case to be test taught before being accepted for publication. Sometimes case publishers do not have a peer-review process but require the case to have been taught a number of times prior to submission (e.g., The Case Centre).

Managing the Peer-Review Process

If your case has made it past the initial case review process from the journal's editor (or a senior member of the editorial team), it will normally be sent out through a blind peer-review process to a number of reviewers who are proficient case writers with subject matter expertise in your area. We have touched on the review process above, but it can be a surprise the first time you submit a case for publication to a case journal. Peer reviewers for case journals take their developmental role very seriously and provide thoughtful, detailed, and often very extensive feedback and suggestions for improving the case and IM/TN. Sometimes this can take the case in a direction not supported by you as the case author. Reviewers can ask for the inclusion of information that is just not available from the organization because either it does not exist, or the organization does not want to disclose it for privacy reasons. The iteration back and forth with reviewers can sometimes take a very long time and require the redrafting of the case a number of times. Each case and IM/TN resubmission should be accompanied by a response to reviewers letter which speaks to what you as the case author have done to specifically address the issues reviewers have raised.

One of the main challenges in case reviews is that reviewers often request additional information to be included in the case, which ultimately makes it longer; this is not an issue for IM/TNs as there is normally no upper limit on their length. The request for new and additional information is particularly problematic if the case has been submitted for a call for short or micro cases. A good journal editor will provide guidance to reviewers to make sure they understand that if they are looking for information to be added to the case, they should also be specific about what can be removed to keep the case narrative at the target length.

Our advice as you work through the review process is to stay positive and remember that you will end up with a more developed case. Remember to keep your tone professional in response to the reviewers' comments and keep track of all the changes you are making in the document as you work through drafts (and save copies of all of the versions). This last piece is particularly important if questioned by a reviewer in a later draft about a change you made in the case or IM/TN when it was in response to a reviewer's request in an earlier version. While it can be tempting to take a break from a case, if you are in the middle of a review process try to make the requested changes as soon as possible after receiving the advice from the reviewers and get it back out for the next round of reviews.

AFTER ACCEPTANCE: WHAT WILL MAKE YOUR CASE SELL

There are a number of elements – outlined in Chapter 2 – that makes a case interesting for students but also for case publishers who look for topical, well-written cases that will interest instructors looking to populate their course with new cases.

Appeal to Instructors

During the publication process, you will be asked to write a short abstract about your case. Make it as interesting and engaging as possible because that is the first thing instructors will read when looking at new cases. Highlight the fact you are covering a hot or evolving topic in their areas, or the refreshed, contemporary way you are presenting a core theory or framework. Make sure you keep to the required case narrative, as the length of a case is always of core interest to instructors and students. Finally, write a robust, inclusive IM/TN to make the instructor's job easier. Go above and beyond – include the links to case supports to make the case come alive in the classroom, teaching timing, board plans, all of the analysis, and if available, an epilogue detailing what happened (e.g., what decision did the company take, what has happened to them since).

Finding your Case

For instructors to adopt your case, they need to be able to find it. Remember to provide specific keywords that allow your case to be more searchable, particularly in the databases of case publishers and distributors. Try to be specific about the targeted level of the case, the general academic area (e.g., marketing, finance, operations management), the topics, theory and frameworks covered, the country and industry in which the case is set, and the size of the focal organization. Some instructors are looking for cases on a specific industry in a specific country so anything you can do to make your case pop up in more searches, the better.

Promoting your Case

Once your case has been accepted for publication, don't be afraid to work with the case publisher to help promote the case. Often case publishers will distribute a number of your cases for free to instructors of your choice in order for it to gain broader exposure. They will also publicize the case through in-person, digital sales and marketing. Often this includes providing free, educator copies of cases once you have proven you are a registered instructor at an academic institution. If you have been published through a case publisher, ask them to use your case as an example when they are presenting or have a booth at academic conferences. If your case adopted the rules in Chapter 2 about what makes the case interesting, they will often be willing to do so because it will attract attention and increase sales. Finally, do not be reticent to reach out to any academic organizations of which you are a part to make them aware of your case, and to use social media to create broader awareness when your case is published.

KEY CHAPTER TAKEAWAYS

- Once you have a final polished case and IM/TN, there are a number of ways for your case to have broader impact. You have first to choose whether you want to publish your case or not.
- If are not interested in publishing your case, you can use it in your classroom to support a particular lesson in your course, use it as an assignment or for an examination, or you can use it as part of an internal student case competition.
- However, many case writers would like to see their case published and can do so through case journals, case publishers, case writing competitions, and textbooks.
- There are a number of steps required to get a case published that are specific to each of the publication outlets. It is very important for case authors to pay close attention to the publisher's requirements for submissions and respect their directions.
- Finally, while the review process for case publication can be long and sometimes frustrating, it is a critical piece to further strengthen your case and IM/TN to make sure it is as effective as possible for the intended audience.

The following chapter provides some final thoughts and strategies to invigorate your case research and writing.

12. Last words on writing cases

The case method has been an integral part of management education for well over a century. In our estimation, the case method is flourishing, with constant demand from around the world for new cases. There are local, country, and global-level case writing communities of practice that have been established and are flourishing. As we have discussed, most cases have a limited shelf life of no more than a decade, so publishing outlets and instructors are constantly looking for great new cases to publish or adopt. New frameworks and theories are being developed which require new cases that give students the chance to practise these approaches. As new markets open and established markets react to industry shifts, there are fantastic opportunities to give students the chance to explore topics in very contemporary settings. Case writing and research therefore represent a huge opportunity for authors like you to make an impact and to publish work that will be used around the world, potentially by thousands of people.

We hope that the background information and advice we have provided so far in this volume have inspired you to become more active in case research. Ideally, by the end of this book we hope you are keen to get started on your next case research project. Some of you may know by now exactly what your next case project is, which is fantastic – good luck and enjoy! For those of you who are excited to get to work but have not yet settled on the direction in which to head, this chapter provides some final helpful tips to help you find your inspiration so you can get started.

LOOK AT YOUR FAVOURITE CASES

One way to get inspired for your next case project is to revisit some of the cases that you love to teach. Nearly every case instructor can point to a case or two that they wish they had written, and they look forward to getting to teach each term. What is it about them that you love? What makes them engaging to students? Why do you think teaching them is important for students? What makes the cases you love to teach different from the ones you don't? As instructors, we know the cases we love to teach, but we do not often stop to consider why we love the ones we do. By identifying the qualities that you love in the cases you use, it can help you figure out what kind of case you want to write. Perhaps you love cases that take place in an industry that is experiencing rapid growth or change. Maybe you love cases about startups that are looking to disrupt how people do things. You might even love cases with captivating protagonists, or those that touch on important social issues. Or maybe you love cases where the focal decision is between two unattractive options. Whatever it is for you, having a good understanding of the cases you love to teach by analysing what it is about them that energizes you is a great place to start in your search for your next case project because then at least you know the effect you are looking recreate.

Another related strategy, of course, is to look at cases that other people love. Most publishing outlets publish lists of their best-selling cases. Reviewing these lists – at least the ones in your discipline – can give you a sense of the current hot topics and what kind of cases are popular. If your goal is to write a best-selling case, knowing what kind of cases are selling well is helpful information. In general, though, we recommend writing cases that speak to you because it is sometimes difficult to predict which cases will become best-sellers, so you might as well enjoy the cases you write. That said, if broad impact is your goal, figuring out what makes for a best-selling case in your discipline is a helpful strategy.

Another strategy is to ask other instructors, colleagues, or case writers about their favourite cases. Getting a broader sense of what others whom you respect think makes a terrific case may help you find your inspiration. It can also introduce you to some potential new cases to add to your course for the future – beyond any you create!

Finally, do not neglect to ask your students – both current and former – what cases resonated for them and why. Students love to give input into courses and will probably give you honest answers about the cases they loved and those they did not. While current students will have opinions, it is good to give it a bit of time from when they analysed the cases to see which cases really resonated with them and why. One method is to ask former students when you see them at graduation which cases they still remember and why. We find this technique is particularly effective with graduate students who have been out working and can reflect on the value of the cases they used in school on their work experiences. Try to look beyond the superficial; we have found that no matter the length, students always feel cases are too long.

The bottom line is that however you manage to figure out what kind of cases excite you and make you want to sit down to start a new project, what matters most is that you learn what motivates you as a case researcher. As you have seen throughout this book, case research can be a long process, so you need to be engaged enough with your work to keep working on it long after the initial enthusiasm has worn off. If you really want to be a case researcher, it is worth investing time into researching, getting feedback about, and analysing the kinds of cases that will be the most rewarding for you to pursue.

LOOK AT WHERE YOU WANT TO PUBLISH

Another strategy to get started on a new project is to begin with your target outlet as your main goal and then determine how you can best contribute to that space. This means reviewing all the publisher's information to authors about the kinds of cases they do and do not publish, as well as their expectations regarding the format for cases and instructor's manuals or teaching notes (IM/TNs). Armed with that information, you can consider how you might develop a case that would match those requirements. It is always helpful as a starting point to read a few recent cases in your field published by that outlet to get a sense of what a finished case looks like there.

There are a few techniques potential authors can use to identify ways to contribute to a particular outlet. The first is to respond to any special calls the outlet currently has available. When an outlet issues a special call, it means they are actively seeking cases of a particular type, usually one that is in demand. They often create special calls to supplement case topics and areas where they feel their catalogue offerings need replenishment. Sometimes special calls relate to case formats (e.g., short cases, secondary source cases). Other special calls relate to certain disciplines, industries, or protagonists (e.g., business ethics, entrepreneurship, or women leaders). If you have the good fortune of having a special call for your target outlet issued for a type of case that you are interested in writing, that is a huge opportunity that you should actively pursue.

However, in the absence of a special call, another strategy is to examine the recent catalogue (i.e., five years old or more recent) of your target outlet and identify any gaps that you might be able to fill. For instance, are there any new research topics in your field that are yet to have many cases written about them (e.g., quiet quitting)? Or are there any organizational issues or practices that have emerged recently that do not have many cases yet available (e.g., post-COVID in-person work policies)? Finally, are there any major external events or social movements that have happened where there are limited cases written about the impacts (e.g., Black Lives Matter, Me Too)? Students and instructors want to use current cases that address the real issues facing contemporary organizations, so if you can find the cutting-edge new issues, you can fill important gaps in an outlet's catalogue. Reviewers and editors also love cases that bring current issues and events into the case literature because they help the outlet and the case method to remain relevant to all users.

If all these approaches do not convince you that you might have a case idea that belongs at your chosen outlet, one last strategy is to contact the editor. You can briefly describe what it is you are considering creating or writing, and request feedback as to whether your project may or may not be a fit for the outlet, or alternatively the conditions under which it would be considered. Some editors may not respond to you, but many will and give you an honest opinion. Most editors would rather redirect an author to another outlet early in the process than have to desk reject or reject a case after first round reviews. Editors of course will not promise authors who write to them for early feedback that their cases will not be rejected later on, but they may help guide authors about whether the idea is worth pursuing and whether an eventual submission would be welcome under their editorship. They can also tell you whether they have a case in their pipeline on their proposed topic that is about to be published so you do not waste your time starting a new case on the same topic. The bottom line is that this approach will not work for every outlet, but there is little downside risk in trying and there can be quite a lot of upsides if you do get a response, even if it is simply not wasting your time with an idea that will not fly at your chosen outlet.

MODEL CASE METHOD

Another technique to help you get started is good old-fashioned mimicry, known as the model case method. Similar to how graduate students are taught to use a model journal research article from their target outlet and structure their own article in the same way, new case authors can also benefit from using this model mimicry method. This method suggests that case authors closely follow the structure and presentation of data in the model case they have selected from the outlet in which they want to publish, writing their own case using the same structure and pattern of presenting data. This approach is just about identifying a case that is similar to the one you want to write and then using that case as a template to produce your own. The advantage of this method for beginners is that it helps with one of the biggest challenges for new case writers – how to structure the presentation of data effectively in a case. With experience, case researchers intuitively understand how to present case data effectively, at which point they can vary the model. However, until that point, a model to follow can greatly improve a new author's first case draft and therefore also improve the response from reviewers as their expectations are more likely to be met.

The model case method is especially effective when learning how to write IM/TNs since they are much longer and more complex than most cases. Moreover, the structure and format of the IM/TN is highly idiosyncratic to each outlet, with little room for authors to vary. Therefore, following a great IM/TN from your target outlet can help authors easily achieve a solid draft that meets expectations. Despite having written dozens of IM/TNs, we both use this method to this day to ensure that our IM/TNs contain all the components that editors and reviewers will want in our work. If you publish in a range of outlets that each have their own strict formats, it is even more helpful to use an appropriate model article because reviewers do not appreciate receiving IM/ TNs in another outlet's chosen format! Following the correct format for your IM/TN is a must as it signals to reviewers that you are serious about doing the work to have your case accepted at that outlet.

REVIEW CASES

Being a reviewer for the outlets within which you wish to publish – including for case conferences – can be an insightful experience. Not only do you get to form your own opinion about the strengths and issues with a submission, but most outlets will share the other reviews with you as well. This information can show you what other reviewers thought about the same case you reviewed, which can be helpful to see what similarities and differences there are in opinions. Thus, being a reviewer can help you understand what reviewers are looking for when evaluating cases. Having a better understanding of the expectations will increase your self-efficacy about case research and improve your odds of having your work accepted.

TEAM UP WITH A CO-AUTHOR

One technique that is worth exploring if you are stuck getting started is to team up with a co-author who is either starting a new case or has one on the go. Most case researchers we know have many more great ideas for cases than they have time to pursue. Teaming up with someone who can advise you when you are unsure of what to do and who can review your work in a developmental manner can put you on the fast track to being a prolific case researcher. So, ask among the case researchers you know and see who could use your help getting their latest project off the ground or ready for submission. Be sure to talk about authorship credit upfront, though, if you do reach out to others.

RECOMMENDED CASE RESOURCES

At the end of this this book we provide a listing of additional case resources for you to explore as you move through your case research journey. There are many case writing organizations, conferences, journals, books and articles, scholarships, training programmes, and case writing competitions that you may wish to investigate. By reviewing this list, you may find an appropriate outlet for your new case, or for your existing work for which you have not yet found a home.

JUST GET STARTED

At the end of the day, becoming a case researcher is something you learn by doing. Both of us wrote our first published case during graduate school simply because the opportunity presented itself to us and we chose to jump at it. We have never looked back and have never stopped since then. Our first cases were not our best work, nor were they even focused on our areas of expertise! But jumping in on low-risk projects is how you learn to research and write a case and IM/TN for publication in a way that works for you.

So, please don't wait too long for the perfect case idea. The best way to learn case research is to just start doing it and keep working on it until you have success or decide it is not for you. We truly hope you end up loving case research as much as we do, and that you find professional impact and satisfaction from your work in this endeavour. If you have read this book, you are likely to have half a dozen great potential case ideas. Pick your favourite, pick up your pen (or turn on your computer), and start telling the story that most interests you. In a year's time, you may find that the story you wrote is helping students from all over the world learn about the topics that matters to you. If you are an academic who cares deeply about student teaching and learning, there are few academic pursuits that are as rewarding and as impactful as case research. We have endeavoured to set you up for success in your own case research and wish you a long career in case research. Thank you in advance for all the many contributions you will no doubt make to the case research field.

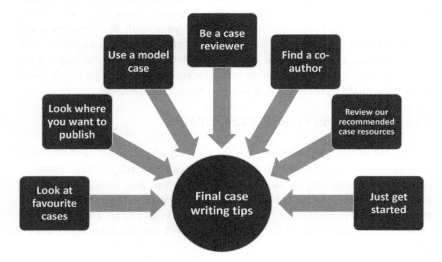

Figure 12.1   Final case writing tips

KEY CHAPTER TAKEAWAYS

- Look at your favourite cases and those of students and colleagues as well as best-selling cases to get inspiration for new case ideas.
- Search the latest issues of your target outlet for gaps you can fill, such as missing or hot new topics, and watch for special case calls.
- Choose an existing case or IM/TN as a model for your new case.
- Be a reviewer for case journals and conferences to learn about how other authors do things and how other reviewers evaluate their work.
- Team up with a co-author to get started and split the work.
- Check out the recommended case resources outlined in the Appendix to this book for additional information.
- Get started on your new case today or submit your existing work somewhere soon.

Appendix: Case resources

This Appendix contains helpful resources for you when considering your future case research and development opportunities. We list suggested books and articles about case writing, organizations that offer resources for case writing, academic conferences that accept cases, academic journals that accept cases, case publishers and distributors, case writing competitions, and case writing scholarships. These are of course the ones of which we are aware, but no doubt there are others as well, particularly regional or discipline-specific case resources. We have provided the full citation or the most current website (as at November 2022) to help you find these resources, but bear in mind URLs can change.

The organizations and associated conferences and journals that we have identified are primarily global ones, but there are also many regional resources. It is worth noting that some organizations (e.g., Harvard Business Publishing) will only directly publish cases created by their own faculty members. However, they have partnership arrangements with other case organizations to distribute their catalogue of cases as well. For example, the *Case Research Journal* distributes its cases through at least nine global case distribution organizations including Harvard Business Publishing, Ivey Publishing, and The Case Centre.

SELECT BOOKS ON CASE WRITING

Andrews, S. (2021). *The Case Study Companion: Teaching, Learning and Writing Business Case Studies.* Abingdon: Routledge.

Beal, B., MacMillan, K., Woodwark, M.J. and Schnarr, K. (2016). *The Case Project Guide: How to Write a Great Business Case as a Class Project.* Ivey Publishing, pp. 1–49 (Guide IM1051) and pp. 1–25 (IM1051TN). Accessed at www .iveypublishing.ca/s/product/the-case-project-guide-how-to-write-a-great-business -case-as-a-class-project/01t5c00000CwltsAAB.

Heath, J. (2015). *Teaching & Writing Cases: A Practical Guide.* The Case Centre.

Morris, R.J. (2022). *The Ultimate Guide to Compact Cases: Case Research, Writing, and Teaching.* Bingley: Emerald Publishing.

Naumes, W. and Naumes, M.J. (2015). *The Art and Craft of Case Writing* (3rd edn). Abingdon: Routledge.

Vega, G. (2022). *The Case Writing Workbook: A Guide for Faculty and Students* (3rd edn). Abingdon: Routledge. Accessed at https://doi-org.libproxy.wlu.ca/10.4324/ 9781003204879c.

Wood, J.D.M., Leenders, M.R., Mauffette-Leenders, L.A. and Erskine, J.A. (2019). *Writing Cases: The Proven Guide* (5th edn). London, ON: Senton Printing.

SELECT ARTICLES ON CASE WRITING

Austin, J. (1993). *Teaching Notes: Communicating the Teacher's Wisdom*. Harvard Business Publishing. Background Note 9-973-105, February. (Revised August 2017.) Accessed at www.hbs.edu/faculty/Pages/item.aspx?num=23299.

Brown, L. and Ettington, B. (2012). Writing an outstanding instructor's manual. *Case Research Journal*, 32(3), 153–9.

Clawson, J. (1995). *Case Writing*. Darden Business Publishing. Technical Note 0033. Accessed at http://store.darden.virginia.edu/case-writing.

Corey, E. (1998). *Writing Cases and Teaching Notes*. Harvard Business Publishing. Background Note 399077, November. Accessed at https://hbsp.harvard.edu/product/399077-PDF-ENG?Ntt=writing%20cases%20and%20teaching%20notes.

Gentile, M. (1990). *Twenty-five Questions to Ask as you Begin to Develop a Case*. Harvard Business Publishing. Background Note 0-391-042, August. Accessed at www.hbs.edu/faculty/Pages/item.aspx?num=11894.

Harris, R., Rowe, G., Grandy, G., Gujarathi, M. and Zadeh, M. (2019). Writing and publishing secondary data cases. *Case Research Journal*, 39(3), 1–15.

Lawrence, J., Guess, K. and Morris, R. (2016). What makes a top selling Case Research Journal case? *Case Research Journal*, 36(1),141–51.

Linder, J. (1990). *Writing Cases: Tips and Pointers*. Harvard Business Publishing. Background Note 391026, August. (Revised April 1994.) Accessed at https://hbsp.harvard.edu/product/391026-PDF-ENG?Ntt=%20writing%20cases%20tips.

Naumes, M. (2013). Writing effective learning objectives. *Case Research Journal*, 33(1), 165–71.

Roberts, M. (2001). *Developing a Teaching Case*. Harvard Business Publishing. Background Note 9-901-055, June. (Revised March 2012.) Accessed at https://hbsp.harvard.edu/product/901055-PDF-ENG?Ntt=developing%20a%20teaching%20case.

Seeger, J. (2012). So, they're writing a case – about you! An open letter to the organizational host of a case writer. *Case Research Journal*, 32(1), 1–6. Accessed at https://nacra.net/wp-content/uploads/2022/04/HA_So_Theyre_Writing_A_Case_About_You.pdf.

Woodwark, M.J. and Grandy, G. (2022). Hey guardians of the case method! Got diversity, equity, and inclusion on your mind? *Case Research Journal*, 42(2), 1–16.

Yemen, G. (2006). *On Writing Cases Well*. Harvard Business Publishing. Background Note UV1290, May. (Revised October 2021.) Accessed at https://hbsp.harvard.edu/product/UV1290-PDF-ENG?Ntt=on%20writing%20cases%20well.

ORGANIZATIONS OFFERING RESOURCES FOR CASE WRITING

Table A.1 lists major case organizations that offer resources for case authors along with a brief description and the current website.

Table A.1   Organizations offering resources for case authors

Organization	Description	Website
Asia Case Research Centre, Hong Kong Business School	Offers resources for case writers	www.acrc.hku.hk/
Emerald Cases Hub	Registration (free) website with videos on how to write a case	https://caseshub.emeraldgroup publishing.com/
Ivey Publishing	Offers resources for case writers and customizable online and in-person case writing workshops	www.iveypublishing.ca/
North American Case Research Association (NACRA) /*Case Research Journal* (CRJ)	Offers articles on how to write cases and IM/TN	https://nacra.net/case-research -journal/articles-on-cases/
Rotterdam School of Management (RSM) Case Development Centre	Offers guided business case writing courses and workshops, case optimization services, and an online case writing guide	www.rsm.nl/cdc/
Society for Case Research (SCR)	Offers a summer bootcamp case writing workshop in conjunction with their annual summer conference	https://bcj.org/
Teaching and Learning Conference (TLC), Academy of Management (AOM)	Regular sessions related to both case teaching and writing	https://aom.org/events/annual -meeting/teaching-and-learning -conference
The CASE Association	Offers the Certified Case Writers Program	www.caseweb.org/certification -program/
The Case Centre	Offers robust case writing resources as well as videos, workshops, webinars, and conference professional development workshops on case writing	www.thecasecentre.org/
The Case Centre, Asia Case Research Centre	Has resources on its website for writing cases	www.thecasecentre.org/ caseCollection/AsiaCaseRese archCentre

ACADEMIC CONFERENCES ACCEPTING CASES

Table A.2 lists major academic case conferences along with a brief description and the current website.

Table A.2   Academic case conferences

Conference	Description	Website
Academy of Management (AOM)	Critical Management Division of AOM accepts cases as part of its annual 'Dark Side of Business' case competition	https://cms.aom.org/awards/new-item3
Administrative Sciences Association of Canada (ASAC)	Peer-reviewed academic business conference with a case track (full cases and cases in development) for cases in English and French	www.asac.ca
International Conference on Information Systems (ICIS)	Accepts teaching cases into its 'Digital Learning and IS Curricula' track (full cases and cases in development)	https://aisnet.org/page/ICISPage
Latin American Council of Management Schools (CLADEA) Business Association of Latin American Studies (BALAS) Case Consortium – International Congress	Peer-reviewed academic business conference with a case track. Cases submitted in Spanish	https://cladea.org/en/home/
North American Case Research Association (NACRA) Annual Meeting	Peer-reviewed academic business conference with pure focus on cases (full cases and cases in development). Has specific tracks for cases written in Chinese, French, Portuguese, Russian, and Spanish	https://nacra.net/
Society for Case Research (SCR) (part of annual Midwest Business Administration Association (MBAA) International Conference)	Peer-reviewed academic business conference with pure focus on cases (full cases and cases in development)	www.ignited.global/scr www.ignited.global/conferences/society-case-research-mbaa-2023

Conference	Description	Website
The CASE Association Annual Meeting	Peer-reviewed academic business conference with pure focus on cases (full cases and embryo cases); held in conjunction with Eastern Academy of Management	www.caseweb.org/
Western Casewriters Association (WCA)	Peer-reviewed academic business conference with pure focus on cases	www.westerncasewriters.org/

ACADEMIC JOURNALS ACCEPTING CASES

Table A.3 lists major academic case journals along with a brief description and the current website.

Table A.3   Academic case journals

Journal	Description	Website
Accounting Perspectives (Wiley – The Canadian Academic Accounting Association)	Peer-reviewed journal accepting cases with an accounting focus. Accept cases in English and French	https://onlinelibrary.wiley.com/ journal/19113838
Asian Case Research Journal (World Scientific)	Peer-reviewed journal accepting factual cases across all business disciplines focused on Asian companies and companies operating in Asia	www.worldscientific.com/ worldscinet/acrj
Asian Journal of Management Cases (Sage)	Peer-reviewed journal accepting factual cases across all business disciplines focused on South, Central, and South-West Asia plus the Middle East	https://journals.sagepub.com/ home/ajc
Business Case Journal (SCR)	Peer-reviewed journal accepting factual cases across all business disciplines	www.ignited.global/scr/ publications/bcj
Case Focus: The Journal of Business and Management Teaching Cases (The Case Centre)	Peer-reviewed journal accepting factual cases across all business disciplines with a focus on the Middle East and Africa	www.thecasecentre.org/ CaseFocus/
Case Research Journal (NACRA)	Peer-reviewed journal accepting factual cases across all business disciplines	https://nacra.net/case-research -journal/

Journal	Description	Website
Emerald Emerging Market Case Studies (Emerald)	Peer-reviewed journal accepting factual cases related to emerging markets and developing economies across all business disciplines	www.emeraldgrouppublishing .com/journal/emcs
IBIMA Business Review (International Business Information Management Association (IBIMA) Publishing)	Peer-reviewed journal accepting cases across all business disciplines	https://ibimapublishing.com/ journals/ibima-business-review/
International Journal of Case Studies in Management (Hautes études commerciales de Montréal – HEC Montréal)	Peer-reviewed journal accepting factual and fictional cases in English and French across all business disciplines with an international focus	www.hec.ca/en/case_centre/ ijcsm/
International Review of Entrepreneurship (Senate Hall)	Peer-reviewed journal accepting factual cases (written and video) with a focus on entrepreneurship	www.senatehall.com/ entrepreneurship
Issues in Accounting Education (American Accounting Association (AAA))	Peer-reviewed journal accepting cases with an accounting focus	https://aaahq.org/Research/ Journals/Issues-in-Accounting -Education
Journal of Accounting Education (Elsevier)	Peer-reviewed journal accepting cases with an accounting focus	www.sciencedirect.com/journal/ journal-of-accounting-education
Journal of Business Case Studies (Index Copernicus International (ICI))	Peer-reviewed journal accepting factual cases related to entrepreneurship	https://journals.indexcopernicus .com/search/details?id=55338
Journal of Business Cases and Applications (Academic and Business Research Institute (AABRI))	Peer-reviewed journal accepting factual and fictional cases across all business disciplines	www.aabri.com/jbca.html
Journal of Business Ethics Education (Philosophy Documentation Center)	Peer-reviewed journal accepting cases related to ethically responsible and culturally sensitive decision-making	www.pdcnet.org/jbee/Journal-of -Business-Ethics-Education
Journal of Case Research (XIM University)	Peer-reviewed journal accepting cases related to organizations and institutions in business, industry, government, non-government and communities	https://xim.edu.in/jcr/
Journal of Case Research and Inquiry (WCA)	Peer-reviewed journal accepting factual cases	https://jcri.org/index.htm

Journal	Description	Website
Journal of Case Studies (SCR)	Peer-reviewed journal accepting decision and descriptive factual cases	www.ignited.global/journal-case-studies-jcs
Journal of Cases on Information Technology (IGI Global)	Peer-reviewed journal accepting factual cases focused on information technology	www.igi-global.com/journal/journal-cases-information-technology/1075
Journal of Critical Incidents (SCR)	Peer-reviewed journal accepting short factual cases that are decision-based or descriptive that discuss an event, an experience, a blunder, or a success	www.ignited.global/scr/publications/jci
Journal of Emerging Technologies in Accounting (AAA)	Peer-reviewed journal accepting cases with an accounting or data analytics focus	https://aaahq.org/Research/Journals/Section-Journal-Home-Pages/Journal-of-Emerging-Technologies-in-Accounting
Journal of Finance Case Research (Institute of Finance Case Research (IFCR))	Peer-reviewed journal accepting cases with a finance focus	www.jfcr.org/jfcr.html
Journal of Information Systems Education (Information Systems and Computing Academic Professionals (ISCAP))	Peer-reviewed journal accepting factual cases focused on information system topics	http://jise.org/
Journal of Information Technology Teaching Cases (Sage)	Peer-reviewed journal accepting decision-based and descriptive cases related to information technology issues	https://journals.sagepub.com/home/ttc
Journal of International Academy for Case Studies (Allied Business Academies (ABA))	Peer-reviewed journal accepting factual or illustrative cases across all business disciplines	www.abacademies.org/journals/journal-of-the-international-academy-for-case-studies-home.html
Journal of International Business Education (Neilson Journals Publishing (NJP))	Peer-reviewed journal accepting decision-based, factual and experience-based cases in the realm of international business. The journal accepts a wide range of case study formats including written paper-based cases, video/film case studies, and software-based cases	www.neilsonjournals.com/JIBE/

Journal	Description	Website
The CASE Journal (TCJ) (Emerald – The CASE Association)	Peer-reviewed journal accepting factual cases in traditional and new forms across all business disciplines	www.emeraldgrouppublishing .com/journal/tcj
The MENA Journal of Business Case Studies (IBIMA Publishing)	Peer-reviewed journal accepting cases across all business disciplines focused on the Middle East and North Africa region	https://ibimapublishing.com/ journals/the-mena-journal-of -business-case-studies/
Vikalpa: The Journal for Decision Makers (Sage – the Indian Institute of Management Ahmedabad)	Peer-reviewed journal accepting cases with a decision-focus across all business disciplines	https://journals.sagepub.com/ home/vik

CASE PUBLISHERS AND DISTRIBUTORS

Table A.4 lists major case publishers and distributors along with a brief description of what disciplines they cover, where they distribute, whether or not they accept cases from outside their own faculty, and the current website.

Table A.4   Case publishers and distributors

Organization	Subject area	Who they distribute	Accept cases from non-faculty?	Website
Asia Case Resource Centre	All business disciplines	HKU	No*	www.acrc.hku.hk/
Centrale de Case et de Médias Pédagogiques (CCMP)	All business disciplines	See: www.ccmp.fr/ distribution/ les-collections -distribuees- -presentation-des -collections	Yes	www.casestudies.ccmp .fr/
Darden Business Publishing	All business disciplines (written, video, multi-media)	Darden Business School cases	No	http://store.darden .virginia.edu/
Harvard Business Publishing	All business disciplines (written, video, multi-media)	See list at: https:// hbsp.harvard.edu/ partners/	No	https://hbsp.harvard.edu/ educator/

Organization	Subject area	Who they distribute	Accept cases from non-faculty?	Website
HEC Montréal Case Centre (Case Catalogue)	All business disciplines with international focus (written, multi-media)	HEC Montreal faculty, International Journal of Case Studies in Management	No	www.hec.ca/en/case _centre/
IBS Case Development Centre	All business disciplines	IBS cases	No	http://ibscdc.org/
IE Publishing	All business disciplines	IE Business School cases	No	https://iepublishing.ie .edu/en/
Insead Publishing	All business disciplines (written, video)	Insead cases	No	https://publishing.insead .edu/
International Institute for Management Development (IMD)	All business disciplines	IMD cases	No	www.imd.org/research -knowledge/case-studies/ case-collections/
Ivey Publishing (Case Repository)	All business disciplines (written, video)	See list at: www .iveypublishing .ca/s/	Yes	www.iveypublishing.ca
Massachusetts Institute of Technology (MIT) Sloan School of Management *(Available for free)*	Accounting; Finance; Entrepreneurship; Leadership; Ethics; Operations; Strategy; Sustainability; System Dynamics	MIT Sloan School of Management	No	https://mitsloan.mit .edu/teaching-resources -library/case-studies
RSM Case Development Centre	All business disciplines (written, multi-media)	RSM cases	No	www.rsm.nl/cdc/ - c27697
SAGE Business Cases	All business disciplines	SAGE cases	Yes	https://us.sagepub.com/ en-us/nam/sage-business -cases

Organization	Subject area	Who they distribute	Accept cases from non-faculty?	Website
Society for Human Resource Management (SHRM) Cases	Limited number of free Human Resource Management cases	SHRM cases	No	www.shrm.org/ certification/for -organizations/academic -alignment/faculty -resources/Pages/Case -Studies.aspx
The Case Centre	All business disciplines (written, video, multi-media, graphic)	See: www .thecasecentre.org/ caseCollection/ default	Yes	www.thecasecentre.org/
Thunderbird Case Studies	All business disciplines	Thunderbird Business School cases	No	https://thunderbird.asu .edu/thought-leadership/ journals-case-series/case -series-listing

Note: * No means that the publisher only accepts cases from its own faculty members – that is, outsider submissions are not accepted even if they are faculty members at other institutions.

CASE WRITING COMPETITIONS

Table A.5 lists major case writing competitions along with a brief description and the current website.

Table A.5   Case writing competitions

Competition	Description	Website
All India Management Association (AIMA) – Indian Case Research Centre (ICRC) Case Writing Competition	Focus on India-focused cases	www.aima.in/events/aima-icrc -case-writing-competition-march -2022
American University Cairo (AUC) School of Business/ Emerald Case Competition	Focuses on developing and emerging economies from authors from the Middle East and North Africa (MENA) region, Pakistan, and Turkey	www.emeraldgrouppublishing .com/publish-with-us/publish -a-teaching-case-study/case -writing-competitions/auc-school -business-case

Competition	Description	Website
Arthur W. Page Society's Case Study Competition	In partnership with the Institute for Public Relations focused on case studies from students enrolled in a school of business, communications, or journalism and who are pursuing a degree that incorporates communications or public relations	https://page.org/study _competitions
Asia Case Writing Competition	Open to authors from Indonesia, Malaysia, Philippines, and Thailand; cases have to focus on developing and emerging markets	www.emeraldgrouppublishing .com/publish-with-us/publish-a -teaching-case-study/case-writing -competitions/asia-case-writing
Association of African Business Schools (AABS)/Emerald Case Competition	Focuses on developing and emerging markets in Africa from authors based at African higher education institutions	www.emeraldgrouppublishing .com/publish-with-us/publish-a -teaching-case-study/case-writing -competitions/aabsemerald-case -writing
China Europe International Business School (CEIBS): Global Contest for the best China-Focused Cases	Focuses on cases in a Chinese business context and open to case developers both inside and outside China. Cases can be in either English or Chinese and include video and other new forms of cases	www.chinacases.org/anon/news/ anon_news_main/anonNewsMain .do?method=listview&fdId =17a570f8b99c4cbe3a1565 842e9986db&docCategoryId =15268313729b7388a323bd c4393895a0&lang=en-US
Diversity, Equity and Inclusion Global Case Writing Competition	Supported by WDI Publishing and University of Michigan's Ross School of Business, this case competition focuses on diversity, equity and inclusion cases	https://wdi-publishing.com/dei -competition-2022/
Emerald/The International Association for Management Development in Dynamic Societies (CEEMAN) Case Writing Competition	Focuses on cases in developing and emerging economies from authors around the world	www.emeraldgrouppublishing .com/publish-with-us/publish-a -teaching-case-study/case-writing -competitions/emeraldceeman -case-writing
European Foundation for Management Development (EFMD) Case Writing Competition	In partnership with The Case Centre, accepts cases from across a broad number of subject categories from global authors	www.efmdglobal.org/awards/case -writing-competition/

Competition	Description	Website
Fox International Business Case Writing Competition	Supported by Temple University's Fox School of Business, the annual case competition has a different theme each year	www.fox.temple.edu/institutes-centers/translational-research-center/activities/fox-international-business-case-writing-competition/
HEC Montréal AEMBA Corporate Social Responsibility Case Writing Competition	Opportunity to write original cases for the Association des Étudiants MBA (AEMBA) Corporate Social Responsibility (CSR) Challenge; cases can be written in either English or French	https://heccsrchallenge.com/csr-case-writing/
Indigenous Voices Case Writing Competition	Focus on original cases that feature an indigenous protagonist or organization and must be written by at least one indigenous scholar	www.emeraldgrouppublishing.com/indigenous-voices-case-writing-competition
John Molson MBA Case Writing Competition	Opportunity to write original cases for the John Molson MBA Case Writing Competition for use in the student case competition; can be written in either English or French	https://mbacasecomp.com/case-writing-competition/
LatAm Business Association of Latin American Studies (BALAS)/Emerald Case Writing Competition	Focuses on original cases from Latin America from authors based at a Latin American business school	www.emeraldgrouppublishing.com/publish-with-us/publish-a-teaching-case-study/case-writing-competitions/latam-balasemerald-case
Program for the Advancement of Research on Conflict & Collaboration (E-PARCC) – Teaching Case and Simulation Competition	Case competition with two tracks: collaborative problem solving, corporate governance, and network governance and analysis; and collaborative methods in international development	www.maxwell.syr.edu/research/program-for-the-advancement-research-on-conflict-collaboration/e-parcc/annual-teaching-case-simulation-competition
TCJ Compact Case Competition	Focuses on original, short cases under 1500 words	www.emeraldgrouppublishing.com/publish-with-us/publish-a-teaching-case-study/case-writing-competitions/tcj-compact-case

Competition	Description	Website
The Case Centre	A number of categories including case writer, outstanding case writer: hot topic, outstanding compact case, and outstanding new case writer	www.thecasecentre.org/AwardsComps/about
The Case for Women	In partnership with The Case for Women, Forté, and MBA Roundtable, this case competition focuses on the female case protagonist	www.emeraldgrouppublishing.com/publish-with-us/publish-a-teaching-case-study/case-writing-competitions/case-women-case-writing

CASE WRITING SCHOLARSHIPS

Table A.6 lists major case writing scholarships along with a brief description and the current website.

Table A.6   *Case writing scholarships*

Organization	Description	Website
Paul R. Lawrence Fellowships, Case Research Foundation (CRF)	Provides fellowships to doctoral students and junior faculty in the first three years of a tenure-track or equivalent appointment to be trained in case research, writing, and teaching at the annual meeting of NACRA	https://caseresearchfoundation.org/
The Case Centre scholarships	Financial support for unpublished Faculty member or PhD student with teaching responsibilities; can be an individual or team	www.thecasecentre.org/caseWriting/scholarships/default

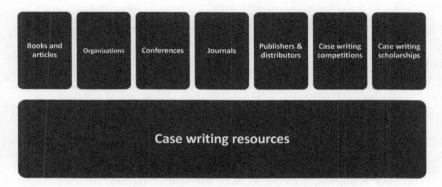

Figure A.1   Case writing resources

KEY APPENDIX TAKEAWAYS

- There are many resources available to case researchers and writers including academic books and articles on the subject.
- There are also quite a few organizations around the world devoted to the development of case research and writing, including many that offer resources for free.
- Academic conferences that have case tracks or accept cases exist in most parts of the world, with most accepting cases from anywhere.
- While there are a couple of dominant players in the case publishing and distribution market (e.g., Harvard Business Publishing, Ivey Publishing), there are a wide range of publishers and distributors who accept open submissions from outside their own organization and several who only accept from their own members.
- If competition is your thing, there are dozens of case writing competitions with open eligibility.
- Finally, if you seek to develop your case research skills, there are a couple of case writing scholarships available to help you develop your practice.

We trust that with all these resources you will be able to develop your case research skills to the fullest and enjoy making your mark on contemporary management education.

References

American Association of Colleges & Universities (AAC&U) (2022). Essential learning outcomes. 25 October. Accessed at www.aacu.org/trending-topics/essential-learning -outcomes.

Andrews, S. (2021). *The Case Study Companion: Teaching, Learning and Writing Business Case Studies*. Abingdon: Routledge.

Austin, J. (1993). *Teaching Notes: Communicating the Teacher's Wisdom*. Harvard Business Publishing. Background Note 9-973-105, February. (Revised August 2017.) Accessed at www.hbs.edu/faculty/Pages/item.aspx?num=23299.

Beal, B., MacMillan, K., Woodwark, M.J. and Schnarr, K. (2016). *The Case Project Guide: How to Write a Great Business Case as a Class Project*. Ivey Publishing, pp. 1–49 (Guide IM1051) & pp. 1–25 (IM IM1051TN). Accessed at www .iveypublishing.ca/s/product/the-case-project-guide-how-to-write-a-great-business -case-as-a-class-project/01t5c00000CwltsAAB.

Berg, N.A. and Fast, N.D. (1975). *Lincoln Electric Co.* Harvard Business Publishing, pp. 1–30. (Revised July 1983.) Accessed at https://hbsp.harvard.edu/product/376028 -PDF-ENG?Ntt=lincoln%20electric.

Boroff, K.E. and Pratt, M. (2017). The incident in Kabul. *Case Research Journal*, 37(4), 1–10. Accessed at https://hbsp.harvard.edu/product/NA0501-PDF-ENG.

Brittain, J. and Sitkin, S. (2008). *Carter Racing* (revised). Dispute Resolution Center, Northwestern University.

Brown, L. and Ettington, B. (2012). Writing an outstanding instructor's manual. *Case Research Journal*, 32(3), 153–9.

Casciaro, T. and Edmondson, A.C. (2007a). *Leading Change at Simmons (C)*. Harvard Business Publishing, 408-062, September. (Revised May 2009.) Accessed at https:// hbsp.harvard.edu/product/408063-PDF-ENG.

Casciaro, T. and Edmondson, A.C. (2007b). *Leading Change at Simmons (D)*. Harvard Business Publishing, 408-063, September. (Revised May 2009.) Accessed at https:// hbsp.harvard.edu/product/408063-PDF-ENG.

Casciaro, T., Edmondson, A.C., McManus, S. and Roloff, K. (2005a). *Leading Change at Simmons (A)*. Harvard Business Publishing, 406-046, November. (Revised May 2007.) Accessed at https://hbsp.harvard.edu/product/406046-PDF-ENG.

Casciaro, T., Edmondson, A.C., McManus, S. and Roloff, K. (2005b). *Leading Change at Simmons (B)*. Harvard Business Publishing, 406-047, November. (Revised May 2007.) Accessed at https://hbsp.harvard.edu/product/406047-PDF-ENG.

Clawson, J. (1995). *Case Writing*. Darden Business Publishing. Technical Note 0033. Accessed at http://store.darden.virginia.edu/case-writing.

Corey, E. (1998). *Writing Cases and Teaching Notes*. Harvard Business Publishing. Background Note 399077, November. Accessed at https://hbsp.harvard.edu/product/ 399077-PDF-ENG?Ntt=writing%20cases%20and%20teaching%20notes.

Dolansky, E. (2019). Snakes & lattes: Playing the marketing strategy game. *Case Research Journal*, 39(1), 1–17. Accessed at https://hbsp.harvard.edu/product/ NA0573-PDF-ENG.

Ellet, W. (2007). *The Case Study Handbook*. Boston, MA: Harvard Business Review Press.

Ellet, W. (2018). *The Case Study Handbook: A Student's Guide*. Boston, MA: Harvard Business Review Press.

Emerald Publishing Group (2022). *The CASE Journal Author Guidelines*. 19 October. Accessed at www.emeraldgrouppublishing.com/journal/tcj#author-guidelines.

Erskine, J.A., Leenders, M.R. and Mauffette-Leenders, L.A. (2003). *Teaching with Cases: The Proven Guide* (3rd edn). London, ON: Senton Printing.

Fairfax, L. and Gong, B. (2022). Expanding the MBA experience by writing and using cases: The student perspective. *Asian Case Research Journal*, 26(02), 189–202.

Galletta, A. (2013). *Mastering the Semi-Structured Interview and Beyond: From Research Design to Analysis and Publication* (vol. 18). New York, NY: New York University Press.

Gentile, M. (1990). *Twenty-five Questions to Ask as you Begin to Develop a Case*. Harvard Business Publishing. Background Note. 0-391-042, August. Accessed at www.hbs.edu/faculty/Pages/item.aspx?num=11894.

Grandy, G. and Ingols, C. (2016). Writing cases about women protagonists: Calling for gender awareness in traditional case portraits. *Case Research Journal*, 36(4), 107–21. Accessed at https://nacra.net/wp-content/uploads/2022/04/WritingCasesaboutWomenProtagonists.pdf.

Gupta, S., Addis, M. and Page, R. (2015). *Eataly: Reimagining the Grocery Store*. Harvard Business Publishing. Accessed at https://hbsp.harvard.edu/product/515708-HTM-ENG.

Hanson, K.O. and Weiss, S. (1991). *Merck & Co., Inc.: Addressing Third-World Needs*. The Business Enterprise Trust, pp. 1–5 (Case 9-991-021) & pp. 1–6 (IM 5-991-025). Accessed at https://hbsp.harvard.edu/product/991021-PDF-ENG.

Harris, R., Rowe, G., Grandy, G., Gujarathi, M. and Zadeh, M. (2019). Writing and publishing secondary data cases. *Case Research Journal*, 39(3), 1–15.

Heath, J. (2015). *Teaching & Writing Cases: A Practical Guide*. Cranfield: The Case Centre.

Herreid, C.F. (2004). Can case studies be used to teach critical thinking? *Journal of College Science Teaching*, 33(6), 12–14.

Ivey Publishing (n.d.). Case and teaching note submission guidelines. Accessed at http://livecontent.ivey.ca/media/24793/ivey-publishing-submission-guidelines.pdf.

Kaw, A. and Hess, M. (2007). Comparing effectiveness of instructional delivery modalities in an engineering course. *International Journal of Engineering Education*, 23(3), 508–16.

Konrad, A. and Phillips, C. (2014). *Vancouver City Savings Credit Union: Working Dads (A)*. Ivey Publishing, pp. 1–4 (Case W14562-PDF-ENG). Accessed at www.iveypublishing.ca/s/product/vancouver-city-savings-credit-union-working-dads-a/01t5c00000CwkGbAAJ.

Lakshminarayanan, S. and Hanspal, S. (2014). Cupcakes by Lizbeth: Flash in the baking pan or here to stay. *The Case Journal*, 10(2), 145–70. Accessed at www.emerald.com/insight/content/doi/10.1108/TCJ-02-2014-0016/full/html.

Lampel, J. (1991). Robin Hood. In A. Thompson, A. Strickland, A. Janes, C. Sutton, M. Peteraf and J. Gamble (eds), *Crafting and Executing Strategy* (19th edn) (pp. 300–301), New York, NY: McGraw-Hill Irwin.

Lawrence, J., Guess, K. and Morris, R. (2016). What makes a top selling Case Research Journal case? *Case Research Journal*, 36(1),141–51.

Linder, J. (1990). *Writing Cases: Tips and Pointers*. Harvard Business Publishing. Background Note 391026, August. (Revised April 1994.) Accessed at https://hbsp .harvard.edu/product/391026-PDF-ENG?Ntt=%20writing%20cases%20tips.

MacMillan, K. (2011). *A Zero Wage Increase Again?* Ivey Publishing, pp. 1–5 (Case 9B11C034). Accessed at www.iveypublishing.ca/s/product/a-zero-wage-increase -again/01t5c00000CwhYoAAJ.

MacMillan, K. and Woodwark, M.J. (2012). *House, Hearth & Home: Managing Leadership Change*. Ivey Publishing, pp. 1–4 (English case 9B12C048), pp. 1–16 (IM 8B12C048). Accessed at www.iveypublishing.ca/s/product/house-hearth-and -home-managing-leadership-change/01t5c00000CwicZAAR.

MacMillan, K. and Woodwark, M.J. (2016). *Somebody Stop the Radio Star: Jian Ghomeshi at the CBC*. Ivey Publishing, pp. 1–5 (Case 9B16C008) & pp. 1–17 (IM 8B16C008). Accessed at www.iveypublishing.ca/s/product/somebody-stop-the -radio-star-jian-ghomeshi-at-the-cbc/01t5c00000CwlaVAAR.

Markulis, P.M. (1985). The live case study: Filling the gap between the case study and the experiential exercise. *Developments in Business Simulation & Experiential Exercises*, 12, 168–71.

Morris, R.J. (2022). *The Ultimate Guide to Compact Cases: Case Research, Writing, and Teaching*. Bingley: Emerald Publishing.

Myrah, K., Rempel, K. and Warner, D. (2021). Addressing homelessness in Kelowna: Determining how a new agency will govern. *Case Research Journal*, 41(3), 1–20. Accessed at https://hbsp.harvard.edu/product/NA0694-PDF-ENG.

Naumes, M. (2013). Writing effective learning objectives. *Case Research Journal*, 33(1), 165–71.

Naumes, W. and Naumes, M.J. (2015). *The Art and Craft of Case Writing* (3rd edn). Abingdon: Routledge.

Prud'homme-Généreux, A., Schiller, N.A., Wild, J.H. and Herreid, C.F. (2017). Guidelines for producing videos to accompany flipped cases. *Journal of College Science Teaching*, 46(5), 40–48.

Rapp, A. and Ogilvie, J. (2019). Live case studies demystified: How two professors bring real-world application to the classroom. Harvard Business Publishing. Accessed at https://hbsp.harvard.edu/inspiring-minds/live-case-studies-demystified.

Risavy, S.D. and Woodwark, M.J. (2020). Mixing business and friendship: A complicated termination decision. *Case Research Journal*, 40(2), 1–12 (Case HBP#NA0639) & pp. 1–33 (IM HBP#NA0640). Accessed at https://hbsp.harvard .edu/product/NA0639-PDF-ENG.

Roberts, M. (2001). *Developing a Teaching Case*. Harvard Business Publishing. Background Note 9-901-055, June. (Revised March 2012.) Accessed at https:// hbsp.harvard.edu/product/901055-PDF-ENG?Ntt=developing%20a%20teaching %20case.

Ross, M., Carayannopoulos, S. and Donovan, M. (2021). TD – Preparing for the future of banking. *Case Research Journal*, 41(1), 1–20 (Case HBP#NA0671) & pp. 1–18 (IM HBP#NA0672). Accessed at https://hbsp.harvard.edu/product/NA0671-PDF -ENG.

Rowe, G. and Schnarr, K. (2012). *The State Fair of Virginia*. Ivey Publishing, pp. 1–20 (Case 9B12M050) & pp. 1–11 (IM 8B12M050). Accessed at www.iveypublishing .ca/s/product/state-fair-of-virginia/01t5c00000Cwi7nAAB.

Rowe, G., Singh-Randhawa, B. and Schnarr, K. (2011). *City Furniture and Mattress*. Ivey Publishing, pp. 1–17 (English Case 9B11M102) & pp. 1–8 (IM 8B11M102).

Accessed at www.iveypublishing.ca/s/product/city-furniture-and-mattress/01t5c00000CwhgoAAB.

Schnarr, K. and Kunsch, D. (2016). *MacPhie & Company: The Growth Imperative*. Ivey Publishing, pp. 1–14 (Case 9B16M133) & pp. 1–13 (IM 8B16M133). Accessed at www.iveypublishing.ca/s/product/macphie-company-the-growth-imperative/01t5c00000Cwlx1AAB.

Schnarr, K. and Rowe, W.G. (2014). *Tim Hortons, Inc.* Ivey Publishing, pp. 1–15 (Case 9B14M114) & pp. 1–11 (IM 8B14M114). Accessed at www.iveypublishing.ca/s/product/tim-hortons-inc/01t5c00000CwkGhAAJ.

Schnarr, K. and Snowdon, A. (2013). *Shriners Hospitals for Children*. Ivey Publishing, pp. 1–11 (English Case 9B13M075) & pp. 1–10 (IM 8B13M075). Accessed at www.iveypublishing.ca/s/product/shriners-hospitals-for-children/01t5c00000Cwj8UAAR.

Schnarr, K., Henriques, K. and Carson, C. (2021). The Briarwood Ballet: An artistic expansion, *Christian Business Academy Review*, 16(1), 11–27.

Schnarr, K., Krizmanich, M. and Lee, C. (2016). *The Kitchener Rangers Hockey Club: Skating into the Future*. Ivey Publishing, pp. 1–15 (Case 9B16M160) & pp. 1–12 (IM 8B16M160). Accessed at www.iveypublishing.ca/s/product/the-kitchener-rangers-hockey-club-skating-into-the-future/01t5c00000Cwm3KAAR.

Seeger, J. (2012). So they're writing a case – about you! An open letter to the organizational host of a case writer. *Case Research Journal*, 32(1), 1–6. Accessed at https://nacra.net/wp-content/uploads/2022/04/HA_So_Theyre_Writing_A_Case_About_You.pdf.

Sharen, C.M. (2016). The balancing act: Making tough decisions. *Case Research Journal*, 36(4), 1–7.

Sharen, C.M. and McGowan, R.A. (2019). Invisible or clichéd: How are women represented in business cases? *Journal of Management Education*, 43(2), 129–73. Accessed at https://doi.org/10.1177/1052562918812154.

Snowdon, A., Schnarr, K. and Kunsch, A. (2014). *Transformational Change at the Centre for Addiction and Mental Health*. Ivey Publishing, pp. 1–13 (Case 9B14M083) & pp. 1–12 (IM 8B14M083). Accessed at www.iveypublishing.ca/s/product/organizational-transformation-at-the-centre-for-addiction-and-mental-health/01t5c00000Cwk1TAAR.

The Case Centre (2022). Submitting multimedia items. Accessed at www.thecasecentre.org/caseWriting/distribution/multimedia.

Tushman, M., Page, R. and Ryder, T. (2010). *Leadership, Culture, and Transition at Lululemon*, multimedia case. Harvard Business Publishing. Accessed at https://hbsp.harvard.edu/product/410705-HTM-ENG?Ntt=.

Vega, G. (2022). *The Case Writing Workbook: A Guide for Faculty and Students* (3rd edn). Routledge. Accessed at https://doi-org.libproxy.wlu.ca/10.4324/9781003204879.

Wood, J.D.M., Leenders, M.R., Mauffette-Leenders, L.A. and Erskine, J.A. (2018). *Learning with Cases: The Proven Guide* (5th edn). London, ON: Senton Inc.

Wood, J.D.M., Leenders, M.R., Mauffette-Leenders, L.A. and Erskine, J.A. (2019). *Writing Cases: The Proven Guide* (5th edn). London, ON: Senton Printing.

Woodwark, M.J. and Grandy, G. (2022). Hey guardians of the case method! Got diversity, equity, and inclusion on your mind? *Case Research Journal*, 42(2), 1–16.

Woodwark, M.J. and Risavy, S.D. (2020). Betting on diversity at Advanced Symbolics Inc. *Case Research Journal*, 40(2), 39–50 (Case HBP#NA0631) & pp. 1–31 (IM

HBP#NA0632). Accessed at https://hbsp.harvard.edu/product/NA0631-PDF-ENG ?Ntt=Woodwark.

Woodwark, M.J. and Schnarr, K. (2022). How to conduct live cases in entrepreneurship education. In K. Wigger, L. Aaboen, D.H. Haneberg, S. Jakobsen and T. Lauvas (eds), *Reframing the Case Method in Entrepreneurship Education: Cases from the Nordic Countries* (pp. 31–9), Cheltenham, UK and Northampton, MA: Edward Elgar Publishing.

Woodwark, M.J. and Wong, M. (2013). *Sawchyn Guitars: Can an Old Business Learn New Tricks?* Ivey Publishing, pp. 1–13 (Case 9B13M084), pp. 1–11 (IM 8B13M084) & pp. 1–2 (IM2 5B13M084). Accessed at www.iveypublishing.ca/s/product/ sawchyn-guitars-can-an-old-business-learn-new-tricks/01t5c00000CwjHeAAJ ?tabset-ce5e5=53fe1.

Woodwark, M.J., Risavy, S.D. and Schnarr, K. (2020a). Doctors divided: The battle over relative physician compensation in Ontario. *Case Research Journal*, 40(3), 89–106 (Case HBP#NA0635) & pp. 1–27 (IM HBP#NA0636). Accessed at https:// hbsp.harvard.edu/product/NA0635-PDF-ENG?Ntt=Woodwark.

Woodwark, M.J., Schnarr, K. and Bes, G. (2020b). *Little Short Stop: Competing in a Shifting Industry.* Ivey Publishing, pp. 1–16 (Case 9B20M076) & pp. 1–12 (IM 8B20M076). Accessed at www.iveypublishing.ca/s/product/little-short-stop -creating-strategy-for-a-shifting-industry/01t5c00000CwpazAAB.

Yemen, G. (2006). *On Writing Cases Well.* Harvard Business Publishing. Background Note UV1290, May. (Revised October 2021.) Accessed at https://hbsp.harvard.edu/ product/UV1290-PDF-ENG?Ntt=on%20writing%20cases%20well.

Yoffe, D. and Kim, R. (2011). *Cola Wars Continue: Coke and Pepsi in 2010.* Harvard Business Publishing, pp. 1–22 (Case 9-711-482), & pp. 1–13 (IM 5-711-531). Accessed at https://hbsp.harvard.edu/product/711462-PDF-ENG.

Index

Printed and bound by CPI Group (UK) Ltd, Croydon, CR0 4YY

16/04/2025

14658489-0005